Other Books by Nancy Flynn

Instant Messaging Rules: A Business Guide to Managing Policies, Security, and Legal Issues for Safe IM Communication, Nancy Flynn, (AMACOM)

E-Mail Rules: A Business Guide to Managing Policies, Security, and Legal Issues for E-Mail and Digital Communication, Nancy Flynn and Randolph Kahn, Esq., (AMACOM)

The ePolicy Handbook: Designing and Implementing Effective E-Mail, Internet, and Software Policies, Nancy Flynn (AMACOM)

Writing Effective E-Mail: Improving Your Electronic Communication, Nancy Flynn and Tom Flynn (Crisp)

E-Mail Management, Nancy Flynn (Thomson Learning)

W9-BSA-647

WITHDRAWN

BLOG RULES

A Business Guide to Managing Policy,
Public Relations, and Legal Issues

NANCY FLYNN

AMACOM

American Management Association

New York • Atlanta • Brussels • Chicago • Mexico City • San Francisco
Shanghai • Tokyo • Toronto • Washington, D. C.

Special discounts on bulk quantities of AMACOM books are available to corporations, professional associations, and other organizations. For details, contact Special Sales Department, AMACOM, a division of American Management Association, 1601 Broadway, New York, NY 10019.
Tel.: 212-903-8316. Fax: 212-903-8083.
Web site: www.amacombooks.org

This publication is designed to provide accurate and authoritative information in regard to the subject matter covered. It is sold with the understanding that the publisher is not engaged in rendering legal, accounting, or other professional service. If legal advice or other expert assistance is required, the services of a competent professional person should be sought.

Although this book is designed to provide accurate and authoritative information in regard to the subject matter covered, it is sold with the understanding that the publisher and author are not engaged in rendering legal, regulatory, technology, or other professional service. The book is presented as a general overview and guide and does not provide legal, regulatory, compliance, technology, communications, or security advice or opinion on any topic contained within. The author of Blog Rules did not and could not contemplate every situation, problem, or issue that may arise when blogging, and this book does not purport to be exhaustive of all situations that may arise when using, implementing, or relying on blog tools and technologies. If legal advice or other expert assistance is required, the services of a competent professional person should be sought.

Library of Congress Cataloging-in-Publication Data

Flynn, Nancy, 1956–
      Blog rules : a business guide to managing policy, public relations, and legal issues / Nancy Flynn.
            p.   cm.
      Includes bibliographical references and index.
      ISBN-10: 0-8144-7355-5
      ISBN-13: 978-0-8144-7355-9
      1. Business communication—Blogs.   2. Customer relations—Technological innovations.   3. Blogs.   4. Corporate culture.   I. Title.

      HD30.37.F59   2006
      659.2—dc22   2006002362

Printing number

10   9   8   7   6   5   4   3   2   1

11/06 R&T 1995

To Paul, Bridget, and Tim.
Thank you, as always, for your patience and support.

CONTENTS

ACKNOWLEDGMENTS

Sincere thanks to those who generously contributed encouragement and support, expertise and information, time and contacts to help make this book possible.

This book would not be possible without the generous gifts of time and encouragement from my husband, Paul Schodorf, and our daughter, Bridget Flynn Schodorf. As always, thank you for your patience and support!

A special thanks to my research assistant Tim Schodorf, for his on-target delivery of valuable information and leads.

Sincere thanks to the following industry experts, professionals, and corporate executives who generously provided time and expertise to help make *Blog Rules* a success: Rick Barry, publisher, MyBestDocs.com; Tim Bray, web technologies director, Sun Microsystems; Christopher Byrne, publisher, ControlsCaddy.com; David Carter, CTO, iUpload; Brian Doyle, corporate affairs director, IBM; Priscilla Emery, president, e-Nterprise Advisors; Casey Flinn, sr. product marketing specialist, St. Bernard Software; Stephen Fronk, attorney, Howard Rice Nemerovski Canady Falk & Rabkin; Jennifer Gazin, associate, LaunchSquad; Christine Halvorson, chief blogger, Stonyfield Farm; Christopher Hannegan, employee engagement practice director, Edelman; Doug Isenberg, attorney, The GigaLaw Firm; Janet Johnson, VP communications, Marqui; Denise Klarquist, VP marketing, Cheskin; Stuart Levi, attorney, Skadden, Arps, Slate, Meagher & Flom; Richard Marshall, attorney, Kirkpatrick & Lockhart Nicholson Graham; Brad Meador, operations VP, ClearContext; Matt Smith, COO, Steve Uhring, sales VP, Amy Dugdale, communications manager, LiveOffice; David Snead, president, W. David Snead, P.C.; Donna Tocci, pubic relations manager, Kryptonite; Steve Wilson, sr. director global web communications, McDonald's.

Thank you to American Management Association (AMA) for their ongoing support of my books and The ePolicy Institute™ through joint programs including AMA/ePolicy Institute™ surveys, forums, and Webinars.

I am grateful to AMACOM books for permission to excerpt material from my previous AMACOM titles *Instant Messaging Rules, E-Mail Rules*, and *The ePolicy Handbook*. I am particularly grateful to Executive Editor Jacquie Flynn for her belief in this book, her patience, and her help in making it happen.

Finally, thank you to the clients, partners, and friends of The ePolicy Institute, www.epolicyinstitute.com, for their ongoing support of our services and programs, including employee training programs, speaking services, expert witness services and litigation consulting, workplace surveys, and policy consulting services.

PART 1

THE CASE FOR STRATEGIC BLOG MANAGEMENT

CHAPTER 1

WHY BLOG RULES?

Blogs are a phenomenon that you cannot ignore, postpone, or delegate . . . blogs are not a business elective. They're a prerequisite.

—*BusinessWeek*[1]

One New Blog Created Every Second[2] . . . Complete with Legal Liabilities and Other Potentially Devastating Business Risks

With a new blog created every second, the hype and hoopla surrounding blogging is understandable. From the millions of individuals with a conviction or cause they are eager to share with like-minded readers, to the thousands of corporations that are looking for a more effective and reliable way to polish reputations and build trust-based relationships with customers, to the bands of citizen journalists who are challenging the mainstream media by offering an alternative news source—everyone, it seems, is blogging.

In spite of the fact that 62 percent of Internet users don't even know what a blog is,[3] blogging has become wildly popular among enthusiasts at home and at the office. Want proof that blogging has entered the culture in a significant and lasting way? *Time* magazine now publishes an annual list of the "50 Coolest Blogs."[4] A few lucky bloggers are invited to walk down the "red carpet" as winners of the Bloggies™, the annual awards ceremony that recognizes the public's favorite blogs and bloggers from around the globe.[5] On a more traditional note, *blog* was added to the venerable *Oxford English Dictionary* in 2003[6] and was the most popular search word in the online version of the *Merriam-Webster's Dictionary* in 2004.[7]

Without doubt, the blog is an electronic communications powerhouse that is likely to have greater impact on business communications and corporate reputations than e-mail, instant messaging, and traditional marketing-oriented websites combined. To quote *Business Week*, blogs are "simply the most explosive outbreak in the information world since the Internet itself. And they're going to shake up just about every business—including yours. . . . Blogs are not a business elective. They're a prerequisite."[8]

> **BLOG RULE #1:** The blog is an electronic communications powerhouse that is likely to have greater impact on business communications and corporate reputations than e-mail, instant messaging, and traditional marketing-oriented websites combined.

Business Can't Afford to View Blogs as "Emerging" Technology

Far from an *emerging* technology that doesn't yet warrant employers' time and attention, blogging is here now; it's here to stay; and it is rapidly—and profoundly—changing the face and voice of business communications. Currently, 89 percent of corporations surveyed either are blogging or plan to do so.[9] About 4 percent of major U.S. corporations currently operate blogs that are *facing out,* or external and available to the public.[10] Among small businesses with fewer than 100 employees, 10 percent have incorporated blogs into their marketing plans, and fully 81 percent report that they plan to increase spending on blogs and other technology tools over the next two to three years.[11]

Many household-name companies currently operate blogs. For example, some 1,500 Microsoft employees write blogs, which are viewable at Microsoft.com/community/blogs.[12] IBM hosts about 2,500 internal blogs on its servers.[13]

It's not just the technology industry that has embraced blogging. The blogging phenomenon has infiltrated all types of businesses in all industry sectors all around the globe. Among professionals, for example, lawyers have been early and enthusiastic adopters of blogging. Legal blogs are so popular that the term *blawg* has been coined to define blogs that are written by lawyers or focus on legal topics.

According to a cover story in *Washington Lawyer*, "Thousands of attorneys, judges, law professors, law librarians, and law students have discovered the promise of blogs."[14] That's fitting, given the tremendous legal liability—including workplace lawsuits alleging copyright infringement, defamation, sexual harassment, and other claims—that is inherent in business blogging.

Business Blogs Are Not Right for Every Organization

A skillfully written, consistently updated, content-rich business blog can be an extremely effective way for organizations to position executives as industry thought leaders, gain the trust of prospective clients and business partners, facilitate productive two-way communication with customers and other important constituencies, enhance media relations, build brand awareness, and nurture valuable relationships with influencers in the blogosphere and beyond.

That does not mean, however, that a blog is a necessary or even an appropriate electronic communications tool for every organization. On the contrary, the blogosphere is an extremely risky environment for business, full of potentially costly legal liabilities and other disasters. Before rushing to establish a business blog, it is essential to consider whether a blog is right for your organization—or whether the legal liabilities and other risks, as well as the commitment of time, talent, and technology associated with blogging, outweigh the potential benefits.

> **BLOG RULE #2**: Business blogs are not necessary or appropriate for every organization. Evaluate the benefits and assess the risks before leaping into the blogosphere.

> **BLOG RULE #3**: Savvy business owners and executives must learn how to strategically and successfully manage the blogosphere today—or risk potentially unpleasant and expensive consequences tomorrow.

Business Blogging 101

The rise of personal blogging has been fast and furious, with an estimated nine million individuals in the United States alone operating weblogs, or blogs.[15] The majority of bloggers use free or inexpensive software, such as

Google's Blogger.com or TypePad.com, for example, to easily and automatically create their blog templates, publish their posts, solicit readers' comments, create all-important incoming and outgoing links, and archive content.

Although personal blogging is booming, the business community has been slower to adopt external blogs as part of the organization's arsenal of electronic communications tools. According to an eMarketer survey reported by the *Wall Street Journal*, only 4 percent of major U.S. companies made external facing-out blogs available to the public in 2005.[16] *Fortune* similarly reports that only 5,000 corporate bloggers were posting commentary for both internal and external readers in 2005.[17]

That said, with the number of blogs doubling every five months,[18] it is a safe bet that corporate blogs will become increasingly common in very short order. In fact, according to a 2005 survey from Guidewide Group and iUpload, 89 percent of organizations are either blogging now or plan to start blogging.[19] Similarly, a survey conducted by Harris Interactive® for HP reveals that 81 percent of small businesses intend to spend more money on blogs and other technology tools over the next few years.[20]

The Power and Popularity of Blogs

1. Every second one new blog, or weblog, is created.[21]
2. Some 80,000 new blogs are created daily, with the number of blogs doubling every five months.[22]
3. By the end of 2005, some 34 million blogs were expected to exist worldwide.[23]
4. Blog search engines track between 15 and 20 million blogs each.[24]
5. In the United States, some 9 million adults publish blogs.[25]
6. Some 32 million Americans identified themselves as blog readers in 2005, representing a 58 percent increase over the previous year.[26]
7. Twelve percent of Internet users have posted comments on blogs.[27]
8. Four percent of major U.S. corporations operate blogs that are facing out, or available to the public.[28]
9. Ten percent of small businesses have incorporated blogs into their marketing plans.[29]
10. In the United States, there are some 5,000 corporate bloggers posting commentary for internal and/or external readers.[30]

11. Fully 89 percent of corporations report that they either are blogging or plan to blog.[31]
12. Forty-four percent of bloggers write new posts at least once a day.[32]

Does Your Organization Really Need a Business Blog?

A blog, or weblog, is a first-person journal that is posted on the web. Blogs can discuss personal topics, professional matters, or a combination of both. A personal blog is an electronic diary in which an individual writer expresses personal (often extremely personal) thoughts and feelings. A professional blog, or a business blog that is hosted by an employer, gives employees the opportunity to comment (positively and negatively) on the organization's people and products, while communicating directly with colleagues, customers, and other third parties. Blogs that combine the personal with the professional result in free-flowing, first-person content in which employee-bloggers write about their own lives, as well as the goings-on inside their companies.

Particularly skillful writers can use corporate blogs to build valuable relationships—and possibly avert public relations disasters—thanks to their willingness to be forthright, transparent, and brutally honest in their commentary. For example, Microsoft's "technical evangelist" Robert Scoble operates Scobleizer, a blog in which he offers daily opinions about the tech world and the inner workings of Microsoft (http://scobleizer.wordpress.com). When Scoble used his blog to acknowledge the blogosphere's growing criticism of Microsoft's new MSN Spaces blogging service, people logged on and listened in.

As reported by *Fortune* (in a cover story identifying blogging as the number-one tech trend to watch in 2005), nearly 4,000 blogs linked to Scobleizer to follow the trusted insider's running commentary on the company's response to the blogosphere's criticism. Scoble, who refers to the blog as "the best relationship generator you've ever seen," has been credited with endowing Microsoft with "an approachable human face."[33]

Who Will Read Your Business Blog?

Like Scobleizer, some blogs are extremely well read, with a devoted following of readers. Slashdot.org, for example, a blog that combines two seemingly unrelated topics, sci-fi movies and open-source software, claims 300,000 to 500,000 readers a day.[34] The blog Arts and Letters Daily (artsand lettersdaily.com) bills itself as a source of intellectual stimulation and attracts 100,000 readers a month, a circulation comparable to the *New York Review of Books'* 115,000 readers.[35] During the 2004 presidential campaign, democratic candidate Howard Dean's campaign blog, blogforamerica.com, drew 100,000 visitors a day.[36]

That said, the majority of business and personal blogs draw a significantly smaller audience, consisting of colleagues and customers, family and friends, and a smattering of readers who either have a personal interest in the blogger's topic, appreciate the blogger's take on a given subject, or simply enjoy the blogger's writing style.

In the blogosphere, the battle for the reader's attention is fierce, as new blogs are being published at the mind-boggling pace of one per second.[37] Although no one knows exactly how many blogs currently exist, the *Wall Street Journal* reports that blog search engines typically track between 15 and 20 million blogs each.[38]

For an idea of what bloggers are writing about, and—unfortunately— what *sploggers,* or spam bloggers, are pitching in the blogosphere, take a look at the new generation of blog search engines, including DayPop (www.daypop.com), Technorati (www.technorati.com), Feedster (www.feedster.com), IceRocket (www.icerocket.com), Bloglines (www.bloglines.com), and BlogPulse (www.blogpulse.com).

Unlike Google, Yahoo, and MSN, which do not allow users to conduct blog-only searches, blog search sites focus solely on the blogosphere, enabling users to find out just what bloggers have to say—about their companies, competitors, employees, or just about any topic you can think of. As reported by *The Wall Street Journal*, these new search engines are designed to "track the information zipping through blogs, nearly in real time."[39]

Two-Way Communication Compounds Risks

Unlike the web, which facilitates the one-way consumption of information, a blog is interactive, featuring the blogger's article, or *post,* and often encouraging comments from readers who are interested in weighing in on a topic to keep the online dialogue going. According to two recent Pew Internet & American Life Project surveys, it is the interactive nature of blogs that appeals to the 12 percent of Internet users who have posted comments or other material on blogs.[40] Ironically, it is precisely the casual, conversational, back-and-forth nature of blogging that makes it both so appealing to blog writers and readers—and so potentially dangerous to business.

BLOG RULE #4: It's the casual, conversational, anything-goes nature of the blog that makes it both so appealing to blog writers and readers—and so potentially dangerous to business.

Everyone who writes a blog and anyone who contributes to a blog's comment section has a voice. Savvy employers should consider managing that voice—for the sake of the organization's reputation and future—either by deactivating or modifying the comment function, editing comments pre-post, or requiring readers to register before posting comments.

This recommendation is likely to spark some outrage among blog enthusiasts who oppose efforts to edit or constrain the unfiltered "honest" nature of blogs. Understood. Bear in mind, however, that the purpose of *Blog Rules* is to provide business readers with an understanding of the best practices, rules, and policies that will help employers manage (and perhaps prevent) blog risks, while taking control of an important business communications tool.

That said, although it may be standard operating procedure for blog publishers to allow anyone—customers, anonymous posters, spam bloggers, former employees with an ax to grind, competitors, and industry critics to name a few—to write freely in response to blog posts, the publishing of unedited, unmanaged comments is simply a bad business practice.

Permalinks Create Permanent Risks

The blogosphere is all about links. Successful bloggers strive to increase traffic and readership by incorporating links into and out of their sites. Thanks to an innovation called the *permalink,* a unique web address is created for every posting on a blog. Bloggers link to one another's posts, which typically remain accessible forever via the permalink (unlike web pages, which are subject to change and removal). The permalink creates a double-edged sword for business, giving blogs "a viral quality, so a pertinent post can gain broad attention amazingly fast—and reputations can get taken down just as quickly."[41]

Blog Rules Is the Business Community's Best-Practices Reference Guide for Managing Blogs

Because you are reading this book, it is likely that your organization is considering taking the leap into the blogosphere to help position your people and products, build your brand and business, or promote a social cause of special significance to the CEO.

Or perhaps your organization has already established a business blog, and now you are eager to learn how to minimize (or perhaps eliminate) the likelihood of workplace lawsuits, trade secret theft, copyright infringement, blog bashings, and other risks through a strategic "best practices" blog management program that is based on clearly communicated blog rules, policies, and procedures.

Regardless of your blogging experience, *Blog Rules: A Business Guide to Managing Policy, Public Relations, and Legal Issues* has you covered. A best-practices guide, *Blog Rules* takes a clear-eyed look at the positives and negatives, risks and rewards, rules and policies of business blogging.

Blog Rules is designed to help organizations of all sizes and industries determine whether blogging is right for their organizations, then—based on that decision—to develop a strategic blog program that helps limit liabilities while enhancing business communications.

Make no mistake. The blogosphere is a scary place for business. In spite of all the hype and publicity surrounding blogs; in spite of all the enthusiasm with which blog writers and their faithful readers approach new posts; in spite of all the real business benefits blogs offer—at the end of the day, blogs pose significant and potentially costly risks to business. Manage business blog risks today, or you may find your organization overcome by potentially expensive (and often preventable) blog-related disasters tomorrow.

Blog Rules Provides Best-Practices Guidelines to Help Limit Liabilities

Because the blog is a relatively new technology that is just starting to make significant inroads into the corporate world, its users are wrestling with a broad range of new challenges and concerns that differ somewhat from those that affect Internet, intranet, e-mail, and instant messaging users.

Blogging is still evolving in terms of its technology, legal and regulatory issues, and overall workplace use, so *Blog Rules* does not always provide hard-and-fast dictates. Instead, this book strives to provide best-practices guidelines for reducing workplace liabilities by proactively managing blog usage, content, and technology.

This book is sold as a general best-practices guide and does not provide advice on legal and regulatory issues or opinions on technology or security. Its author did not and could not contemplate every situation, problem, or issue that may arise when blogging.

Before acting on any issue, rule, policy, or procedure addressed in *Blog Rules*, you should consult with professionals competent to review the relevant issues.

Some organizations and industries may be required to adhere to different or additional rules and regulations from those described in *Blog Rules*. You should contact a professional for advice about the specific risks, regulations, rules, and policies governing your particular business and industry.

Recap and Blog Action Plan

1. With one new blog created every second and 89 percent of corporations reporting that they currently blog or plan to do so, the blog is an electronic communications powerhouse that is likely to have more impact on business communications and corporate reputations than e-mail, instant messaging, and traditional marketing-oriented websites combined.

2. Employers cannot afford to dismiss the blog as an emerging technology that doesn't yet warrant consideration. Blogging is here now, and it's here to stay.

3. A skillfully written, regularly updated, content-rich business blog can be an extremely effective way for organizations to position executives as industry thought leaders, gain the trust of customers, and facilitate productive two-way communication with colleagues, clients, and other important constituencies.

4. The blogosphere is an extremely risky environment for business, full of potentially costly legal liabilities and other disasters. Before rushing to establish a business blog, consider whether the risks outweigh the potential benefits.

5. The blog is interactive, featuring the blogger's article, or post, and often encouraging comments from readers who are interested in weighing in on a topic to keep the online dialogue going. Ironically, it is the casual, conversational, back-and-forth nature of blogging that makes it both so appealing to blog writers and readers—and so potentially dangerous to employers.

6. Responsible employers are obligated to take control of business blogging. Establish written rules and policies to help prevent (and in some cases eliminate) the risk of litigation, regulatory violations, and other blog-related disasters.

7. Seek the advice of competent legal, regulatory, records management, IT, security, public relations, and human resources experts before implementing rules, policies, and procedures for your business blog.

CHAPTER 2

BLOGS POSE UNPRECEDENTED RISKS TO BUSINESS

There's no escaping the blog. Freewheeling bloggers can boost your product—or destroy it. Either way, they've become a force business can't afford to ignore.

—*FORTUNE*[1]

Is competitive pressure driving your organization to consider blogging? On the one hand, it's certainly true that an organization without an external blog may risk losing position, market share, reputation, and sales to tech-savvy competitors who have already recognized—and tapped into—the power of the blogosphere.

On the other hand, it's also true that no corporate blog means no blog-related lawsuits or other potentially costly and time-consuming liabilities. That's good news, considering how ill-prepared many employers are to manage employee blogs.

> **BLOG RULE #5:** An organization without an external blog program may risk losing position, market share, reputation, and sales to tech-savvy competitors who have already recognized—and tapped into—the power of the blogosphere.

The strategic management of blogs (or any other electronic business communications tool) begins with the establishment of written rules and policies governing usage (at the office and at home) and content (employee posts and reader comments). Unfortunately, when it comes to blogging, rules and policy have not yet caught up with ease of use and popularity.

> **BLOG RULE #6:** The strategic management of blogs or any other electronic business communications tool begins with the establishment of written rules and policies governing usage and content.

Although the majority of employers are using policy to help manage employees' e-mail and Internet use, the same cannot be said of workplace blogging. Surveys conducted by American Management Association and The ePolicy Institute reveal that fully 79 percent of organizations have implemented e-mail policies,[2] and another 81 percent have established rules governing personal Internet use.[3] That's more than double the 30 percent of organizations that have instituted policies to govern employee bloggers, according to a 2005 survey by communications giant Edelman.[4]

Of the organizations that have implemented written blog rules, merely 23 percent use policy to control personal postings on corporate blogs, and just 20 percent have implemented written rules to manage the operation of personal blogs on company time, according to the 2005 Electronic Monitoring and Surveillance Survey from American Management Association and The ePolicy Institute.[5]

Blogs Policies Trail Workplace Blog Use

With one new blog created every second,[6] and blog search engines now tracking up to 20 million blogs each,[7] the likelihood that some of your employees, customers, suppliers, ex-employees, shareholders, competitors, industry influencers, and other members of your corporate community are blogging is very real.

In spite of the boom in blogging and the potentially costly risks associated with unmanaged content, employers have been slow to implement rules and policies designed to control what employee-bloggers may—and may not—write about the organization, its people, products, and services.

As the facts demonstrate, most employers are ill-prepared to manage business blog usage and risks:

1. Only 30 percent of organizations have instituted blog guidelines or policies.[8]

2. Merely 23 percent of companies use written policy to control personal postings on company blogs.[9]
3. A scant 20 percent of employers have established rules and policies to manage the operation of personal blogs on company time.[10]

The absence of blog rules is a potentially costly oversight. As Edelman and Intelliseek detail in their white paper, "Talking from the Inside Out: The Rise of Employee Bloggers," within organizations that operate business blogs, "employees at all levels have suddenly found themselves in powerful positions to advocate either for or against their companies' products, policies, and stances—and have found that people are listening to what they have to say."[11]

Giving employees free rein over corporate communications—without strategic blog-related rules, policies, procedures, training, and technology in place—puts the organization at tremendous risk. Some blogs attract hundreds of thousands of readers a day—day after day. Do you really want your employees communicating with an audience that large without the benefit of comprehensive rules, clearly written policy, and formal training? Are you willing to risk having unmanaged and untrained employee-bloggers talk about your business, engage your customers, and accidentally (or intentionally) reveal top-secret company information?

BLOG RULE #7: A business blog opens the organization up to potential disasters, including the loss of trade secrets, confidential information, and intellectual property; negative publicity, damaged reputations, and public embarrassment; workplace lawsuits alleging copyright infringement, defamation, sexual harassment, and other claims; court sanctions, legal settlements, and regulatory fines; and lost employee productivity.

Before Rushing to Establish a Business Blog, Consider the Risks

In spite of blog enthusiasts' encouragement to "Come on in, the blogging's wonderful,"[12] the truth is that blogging poses risks to everyone—employers, employees, and even individual bloggers. Hundreds of employees have been *dooced,* or fired, from their jobs for blogging—often on their own time using their own computers in the privacy of their own homes (see Chapter 13 for the story behind the term *dooced*). A few high-profile personal bloggers have been the targets of embarrassing media coverage when their extremely private blogs have unintentionally gone public. Now we are starting to see individual bloggers being hit with lawsuits stemming from the content they and their readers are posting.

While an employee who has just been dooced for publishing catty comments about the boss may not agree, the fact is that the dangers blogging poses to individuals do not compare to the risks faced by employers who opt to host company blogs—particularly if they do so without written rules, policies, and procedures in place.

What Makes Blogging So Dangerous for Business?

There are plenty of reasons for organizations to approach blogging—cautiously—as a relatively easy, inexpensive, and (potentially) effective way to share information among employees, demonstrate thought leadership, troubleshoot problems, create an ongoing dialogue with customers, and build valuable relationships with important constituencies, including influential bloggers.

Employers should be mindful, however, that heightened regulatory oversight and a highly litigious business environment bring new and potentially costly challenges to corporate blogs. The accidental misuse (and intentional abuse) of business blogs by employees or malicious third parties can create potentially expensive and time-consuming legal, regulatory, security, public relations, and productivity headaches for employers. Unfortunately, management, technology, and the legal system have not yet caught up with the potential benefits and risks of business blogging.

BLOG RULE #8: Management, technology, and the legal system have not yet caught up with the potential benefits and risks of business blogging.

By now, most workplace computer users are aware of the countless high-profile e-mail, IM, and Internet gaffes that have triggered everything from tumbling stock prices to seven-figure legal settlements to billion-dollar regulatory fines to media feeding frenzies. Why assume blogging will not exact an equally high toll on the business community?

Consider a Few of the Risks Blogs Pose to Business

1. Litigation Risks: Copyright Infringement, Invasion of Privacy, Defamation, Sexual Harassment, Hostile Work Environment Claims, and Other Legal Risks

As detailed in Part 2, bloggers' posts and readers' comments open the organization up to a broad range of legal risks and create a new pool of electronic evidence for prosecutors and litigators to dive into.

2. Security Breaches: Loss of Trade Secrets, Confidential Information, Intellectual Property

More than half of all employers surveyed (57 percent) are concerned about employees exposing sensitive company information on blogs, according to a Forrester and Proofpoint survey.[13] No wonder growing numbers of companies are using firewall technology to block employees' access to third-party, outside blogs,[14] where they could easily post comments that accidentally (or intentionally) expose trade secrets, reveal corporate financials, or otherwise disclose confidential company information.

3. Discovery Disasters: Mismanagement of Electronic Business Records

On company-sponsored blogs, employee writers and third-party commenters may be creating electronic business records that the company is obligated to formally save and store.

Nearly a third of bloggers surveyed (32 percent) by Edelman and Technorati report that their primary reason for blogging is to "create a record of my thoughts."[15] Ironically, that record could be used as evidence for—or against—the blogger and the blogger's employer should a workplace lawsuit be filed and blog posts be subpoenaed.

4. Public Relations Nightmares: Blog Storms Sink Corporate Reputations

Anyone with a computer and Internet access (or a cell phone) can create a blog and start posting commentary—including negative, critical, or defamatory remarks about any individual or organization—within minutes. More than 50 percent of bloggers surveyed report that they write about companies, their products, or employees at least once a week.[16]

Orchestrated attacks in the blogosphere have tarnished corporate reputations, defamed individuals, disabled corporate operations, cost millions in lost revenues, and terrified the employees and families of individual scapegoats. According to one legal expert, at least half of all blog attacks are sponsored by competitors eager to destroy business rivals by unleashing the fury of the blogosphere.[17]

5. Loss of Control: Real-Time Broadcasting of Information Can Be a Risky Proposition for Business

Fear of losing control of the company message has stopped 22 percent of employers surveyed from adopting a business blog. Another 22 percent report that they have steered clear of business blogs because of their concerns about what employees might say.[18]

6. Productivity Drains: Bloggers Log On and Slack Off

Whether blogging for business or personal reasons, employees are devoting (and often wasting) a tremendous amount of time reading, writing, and commenting on blogs. About 35 million workers, or one in four employees, spend 3.5 hours, or 9 percent of the work week, in the blogosphere, according to an *Ad Age* "best-guess" analysis of blog-related surveys and data.[19]

In dollars and cents, what does all that non–work-related blogging actually mean to employers? According to a 2005 employee productivity survey conducted by America Online and Salary.com, the average American worker wastes two hours a day on non–work-related activities, with 45 percent of slackers reporting that their number-one goof-off activity is surfing the Net for personal reasons. The cost of all that slacking (online and otherwise) is a whopping $759 billion in lost productivity annually.[20]

7. Regulatory Violations: Risks to Publicly Traded and Regulated Companies

As detailed in Chapter 8, unmanaged blog content could land a publicly traded company or regulated firm in hot water with the Securities and Exchange Commission (SEC), National Association of Securities Dealers (NASD), New York Stock Exchange (NYSE), or other federal, state, local, and industry regulators.

8. Spam + Blog = Splog: Spam Invades the Blogosphere

It should come as no surprise to anyone that spam, in the form of comment spam and splog, has invaded the blogosphere.

If you allow employees to use free or inexpensive blog creation software and hosting services, then you open your organization to splog and comment spam. Just as free, public instant messaging clients make organizations vulnerable to security risks, so too do free, public blog tools and services. Organizations that are concerned about managing blog risks are advised to use enterprise blog technology that is designed to help manage content and control risks.

Recap and Blog Action Plan

1. The strategic management of business blogs begins with the establishment of written rules and policies governing professional and personal use, along with the type of content that employees, customers, and other third parties may post.

2. Giving employees free rein over corporate communications—without strategic blog-related rules, policies, procedures, training, and technology in place—opens the organization up to potential disasters, including the loss of trade secrets, confidential information, and intellectual property; negative publicity, damaged reputations, and public embarrassment; workplace lawsuits alleging copyright infringement, defamation, sexual harassment, and other claims; court sanctions, legal settlements, and regulatory fines; and lost employee productivity.

CHAPTER 3

START WITH A CLEAR OBJECTIVE: WHY BLOG?

Potential customers are out there, sniffing around for deals and partners. While you may be putting it off, you can bet that your competitors are exploring ways to harvest new ideas from blogs.

—BusinessWeek[1]

Because blogging is so easy, inexpensive, and potentially effective as a business communications tool, you may be tempted to leap immediately into the blogosphere. Not so fast. Before your organization joins the 4 percent of major U.S. corporations that have already established external, facing-out blogs,[2] take time to assess the risks, evaluate the benefits, and develop a strategic approach to blog program development and management.

BLOG RULE #9: Strategic blog management begins with the establishment of a clear objective. In other words, why does your organization want to blog?

Define the Mission of Your Corporate Blog

Successful business blogs tend to be narrowly focused, concentrating on a specific topic, and tend to be written by one individual. If, in the course of the self-assessment process, the blog management team determines that the organization has multiple blogging goals, various messages to communicate, and diverse audiences to engage, then you will probably want to operate more than one business blog.

Typical reasons for launching a business blog program include:

1. To lend a human face and voice to an otherwise cold and impersonal organization.
2. To help position the CEO and other senior executives as *thought leaders,* expert sources of information about the company, the industry, and the business community in general. Fully 61 percent of business bloggers say they use external blogs mainly to demonstrate thought leadership.[3]
3. To "warm up" the image of the CEO, establishing the fact that the CEO is friendly and approachable—a "regular" person speaking in a "regular" voice. A word of caution, however. A CEO blogger must be ready, willing, and able to post copy on a regular basis— ideally once a day, just as 44 percent of all bloggers do.[4] The CEO, like any employee-blogger, also must be prepared to manage and respond to all the reader comments and e-mail messages that a high-traffic blog (or even a less-well-read blog) generates.
4. To enhance communications with customers and prospects by creating a vehicle for two-way communications via writers' posts and readers' comments. Among organizations that operate external blogs, 35 percent report that they use blogs to maintain regular communication with partners and customers.[5]
5. To create an easy and accessible technical-support tool. Employee-bloggers write tech-related posts, and customers/tech users submit questions, complaints, praise, concerns, and so on in the form of blog comments.
6. To enhance internal communications among employees. Internal blogs provide organizations with a terrific knowledge-sharing tool, as work teams and departments hold password-protected conversations online.
7. To enhance the organization's public relations (PR) efforts, giving the PR team an additional communications channel (employees' posts written in each employee-blogger's own words and writing style) to deliver important company messages to customers, bloggers, and other influential audiences. Fully 61 percent of businesses that operate external, or facing-out, blogs report that they do so mainly for public relations and marketing purposes.[6]
8. To help promote a brand, product, or service to consumers who turn to the Internet, including blogs, to research companies and products.

9. To promote a social cause of importance to the CEO, the organization, and the community.

10. To establish an open and ongoing dialogue with important communities, including employees, prospective employees, customers, prospective customers, suppliers, the media, the business community, government officials, the general public, business partners, and prospective business partners, among others.

11. To improve brand recognition. The majority (78 percent) of organizations that operate blogs to communicate with external audiences cite "improved brand recognition" as the number-one benefit to be gained.[7]

12. To leverage content across marketing channels. Organizations can use blog posts to drive readers to corporate websites, survey summaries, news articles, white papers, press releases, brochures, event calendars, executive bios, and other content that the organization may want to put in front of readers' eyes.

13. To conduct polls and receive immediate feedback. When organic yogurt manufacturer Stonyfield Farm began searching for a pediatrician to partner with, the company polled readers of its Baby Babble blog to determine which pediatricians were most trusted by parents of infants and young children. The feedback was immediate and led Stonyfield Farm to a potential pediatrician-candidate. Had the company relied on a traditional telephone survey or onsite focus groups, the fact-finding process might have dragged on for weeks.

14. To gather customer feedback. Fully 66 percent of those surveyed cite "customer feedback" as one of the primary benefits of business blogging.[8] You can use the comment section of employees' blogs to get this job done. Or, consider posting customers' questions and comments, along with employee-bloggers' responses, on a FAQ-type blog page.

15. To pursue advertising and sponsorship possibilities. The 2005 "Blogging In the Enterprise" survey from Guidewire Group and iUpload reveals that 20 percent of organizations expect external business blogs to generate income.[9] According to *BusinessWeek*, popular blogs can land sponsorship deals that are worth as much as $25,000 a month.[10]

16. To keep pace and protect company assets. Writing in the *Harvard Business Review*, Sun Microsystems president and COO Jonathan Schwartz warned executives, "In ten years, most of us will communicate directly with customers, employees, and the broader

business community through blogs. . . . If you're not part of the conversation, others will speak on your behalf—and I'm not talking about your employees."[11]

17. To build relationships with strategic partners. Consider inviting a business partner to contribute a post to your blog as a guaranteed way to solidify ties with your guest blogger.

18. To replace opt-in e-mail distribution lists and mass e-mail broadcasts with business blogs. Blogs enable the organization to easily deliver (and update) information to internal and external readers. If you need to update or change information, there is no need to rebroadcast a message (unlike e-mail). Simply update your blog post, and readers will see it when they return to your site.[12]

19. To keep in touch with subscribers who get pinged when you update your blog. Ping services like weblogs.com automatically alert subscribers when new content is added to a blog. That's one more good reason to update blog content regularly—ideally once a day.

20. To generate awareness of and buzz about products and services. "Regular people" (including customer evangelists and nonexecutive employee-bloggers) are viewed as three times more credible than established authority figures, according to a 2005 Blogger Survey from Edelman and Technorati.[13] According to another recent survey, one third of all consumers would prefer to receive product information from friends and specialists, rather than advertisers.[14]

21. To respond immediately to whatever issue or event your organization chooses to take a stand on or voice an opinion about. Whether it is breaking news, a change in the law, election results, or product announcements, your business blog program means you can post an immediate response. No issuing press releases. No calling reporters. No hoping your executives will be chosen for media interviews.

22. To communicating with the media. According to a survey from EURO RSCG Magnet and Columbia University, more than 28 percent of journalists rely on blogs for reporting and research. Fully 70 percent of journalists surveyed say they have turned to blogs to find story ideas, research and reference facts, locate sources, and uncover breaking news.[15]

23. To gain insight into how employees really feel about the company and the boss. To quote the *New York Times*, "A blog can be a great way to vent about work." Unfortunately for some employees, "It can also be an invitation to a pink slip."[16]

24. To attract search engines. Search engines like blogs, thanks to their keyword-rich and regularly updated content, combined with numerous inbound and outbound links. A business blog with a high search engine ranking will help attract visitors to the organization's corporate website and generate increased interest in the company and its products overall.

25. To recruit employees. A blog makes the organization seem "cool." For younger employees, for whom blogging is a way of life, the presence of a business blog program may be particularly attractive.

Develop a Strategic Management Plan to Fit Your Blog's Objective

According to a Backbone Media survey, there are five main reasons why businesses operate blogs:

1. Publish content and ideas: 52 percent
2. Promote thought leadership: 48 percent
3. Build a community: 46 percent
4. Deliver information quickly to customers: 34 percent
5. Receive feedback from customers: 21 percent[17]

Once your organization has determined why it wants to blog, you can get to work developing your organization's strategic blog management plan. Here are some points to consider:

- Does the company plan to operate internal (employees' eyes only) or external (customer facing-out) blogs?
- Are your employees prepared to devote the time necessary to write, update, and maintain business blogs? That includes responding to the comments and e-mail that blogs, particularly well-read high-traffic blogs, can generate.
- Do employee-bloggers have the writing skills necessary to create the type of compelling, readable blog content that keeps readers coming back for more?
- Is your CEO really prepared to do what it takes (researching, writing, updating, and responding to comments and e-mail) to be a successful blogger?
- Is your business blog likely to find a following quickly enough to justify start-up time and operational expense?

- Have your blog management team and legal counsel thoroughly researched the potential business, legal, and regulatory risks associated with blogging?
- Does your company possess the technology expertise necessary to identify, evaluate, and install blog content management, blog monitoring, and blog security tools?

Before launching headfirst into a business blog program, employers are encouraged to work through the comprehensive "Self-Assessment for Would-Be Business Bloggers" in Chapter 4. Ideally, your responses will shed some light on your organization's preparedness to undertake a blogging initiative.

Recap and Blog Action Plan

1. Strategic blog management begins with the establishment of a clear objective. Before launching into the blogosphere, first determine why your organization wants to blog, what benefits a business blog program can bring to your organization, and what risks the organization must be prepared to avert or overcome.
2. Assign your organization's blog czar or blog management team the task of determining if blogging is right for your organization, and—if it is—to define the mission of your corporate blogging program.
3. Carefully weigh blog risks against business benefits before undertaking a business blog initiative.

CHAPTER 4

PROCEED WITH CAUTION

Self-Assessment for Would-Be Business Bloggers

Blogging can kill you. Before, when we had a problem, it was addressed in the public media. Now the Internet is many times faster, more unforgiving and out of control.

—Crisis Management International CEO Bruce T. Blythe,
quoted in *Marketing Wharton*[1]

For employers who are still challenged by workplace e-mail, instant messaging, and Internet management, blogs pose new and potentially costly risks. Unmanaged weblogs put the organization's assets, reputation, and future at risk. Without strategic blog-related rules, policies, and procedures in place and consistently enforced, employers face numerous electronic disasters, including the loss of trade secrets, confidential information, and proprietary data; negative publicity, tarnished reputations, and public embarrassment; workplace lawsuits and regulatory fines; security breaches including comment spam and splog (spam blog) attacks; and lost productivity, among other risks.

Self-Assessment Questionnaire

To help avert blog-related disasters, while maximizing the potential benefits of business blogging, complete the following self-assessment to determine your awareness of blog-related liabilities and better understand the ways in which *Blog Rules* can help your organization manage blog risks.

1. Has your organization established a blog management team to oversee the development and implementation of your blog rules, policies, and procedures?　Yes _____ No _____

2. Has your blog management team determined a clear objective for your corporate blogging program?　Yes _____ No _____

3. Has your organization developed and implemented a strategic blog management program that combines written blog policy and formal employee education?　Yes _____ No _____

4. Has your company put into place blog-related policies and procedures designed to keep confidential information secure, corporate financial data reliable, trade secrets under wraps, and nonpublic data private?　Yes _____ No _____

5. Has your organization developed a procedure for handling violations of its blog content and usage policy?　Yes _____ No _____

6. Is your company publicly traded?　Yes _____ No _____

7. Is your company a health care organization that is governed by Health Insurance Portability and Accountability Act (HIPAA) regulations?　Yes _____ No _____

8. Do you plan to allow customers and other third parties to post comments on your business blogs?　Yes _____ No _____

9. Are you prepared to review all content and comments before they are posted on corporate-sponsored blogs to help ensure that your company does not run afoul of laws and regulations?　Yes _____ No _____

10. Does your organization have in place a policy governing the retention of electronic business records, including blog posts and readers' comments?　Yes _____ No _____

11. Do you really want to provide employees, customers, disgruntled former employees, competitors, and others with a public forum (in the form of the comment sections of employees' business blogs) to discuss, challenge, criticize, and complain about your business?   Yes _____ No _____

12. Do you have the time and resources (financial and human) to monitor what is being written about your organization on employees' company-hosted blogs, employees' personal blogs, and third-parties' blogs?   Yes _____ No _____

What Your Responses Mean

1. Establish a Blog Management Team

Don't assign one individual the responsibility of single-handedly developing and implementing your organization's business blog program. To help mitigate risks and to ensure that your business blog program meets the organization's management, legal, regulatory, and communications needs, assign a blog management team that is made up of some or all of the following professionals.

• *Blog Czar.* The team leader of the organization's strategic blog program, the blog czar keeps the blog management team on track and ensures the timely development and implementation of strategic blog rules, policies, and procedures. The blog czar also sends a clear signal to the staff that the organization is fully committed to its strategic blog program and expects 100 percent compliance from employees.

• *Senior Executive.* In addition to a dedicated blog czar, you can increase the likelihood of blogging success by appointing a senior executive to champion your blog risk-management program and team. With the right champion leading the charge, your blog management team should have little trouble receiving support, funding, and possibly even the participation of the CEO and other company decision makers.

• *Legal Counsel and Compliance Officer.* Legal and regulatory compliance is integral to successful blog risk management. Have your legal counsel review the blog-related risks, rules, regulations, and responsibilities facing your business and industry. Your legal and compliance officers should work together to ensure that all relevant federal and state laws are adhered to, and government and industry regulations are addressed in your blog policy.

Your legal and compliance officers also should be involved, along with the organization's records manager, in the development and implementation of the organization's retention and archiving strategies to ensure that blog posts and reader comments that create electronic business records are properly saved and stored. In addition, assign your legal and compliance team the task of supervising litigation response to ensure that blog records can quickly and reliably be located and produced, should your organization be hit with a subpoena from a court or regulator.

- *Records Manager.* Many forward-thinking organizations employ a records manager to ensure that both paper and electronic business records, including e-mail messages, instant messages, and the history of employees' Internet activity, are properly retained and archived. The objective is to ensure that the organization is able to produce subpoenaed business records in the event of a workplace lawsuit or regulatory investigation.

Don't forget to include blog posts and comments in your organization's electronic records retention plan, as well. Blogs posts that are written by employees and executives, as well as the comments that are offered by customers and other third-party readers, may produce business records that your organization is obligated to retain for business, legal, and regulatory reasons.

- *Human Resources Manager.* Since your HR manager is likely to be responsible for educating employees about the company's blog rules and policy, as well as disciplining (and perhaps terminating) blog policy violators, be sure to include the human resources department in the development and implementation of the organization's blog rules, policies, and procedures.

- *Chief Information Officer.* Your CIO can help bridge the gap between people problems and technology solutions. IT professionals can play an important role in identifying blog risks and recommending the most effective enterprise technology tools to help control and manage content, retain and archive business records, block employee access to external blogs, and otherwise help manage the organization's blog risks.

- *Public Relations Manager.* Whether your organization is contemplating the establishment of its own business blog or wants to take proactive steps today to avoid a potential bashing in the blogosphere tomorrow, it is essential to involve its public relations team in the blog management mix— right from the beginning.

• *Customer Service Manager.* For some companies, the blogosphere is a customer service dream, generating goodwill among satisfied consumers who appreciate the two-way communication created by the blog, and reaping positive comments from satisfied customers who are happy to salute your company for a job well done.

Not all organizations are that lucky, however. On the contrary, the blogosphere can be a customer service nightmare for organizations that simply choose to ignore postings that are critical of the company's products or its responsiveness to customer complaints.

Ignore customer complaints today, and you are likely to discover that "I hate your company" blogs have popped up overnight. Thanks to the permalink, posts remain archived and available forever. Thousands (possibly millions) of your customers (along with the media) can hop from one gripe site to another, reading about your "terrible" company, its "inferior" products, and its "lousy" service. To help prevent this type of blog-based disaster, assign your organization's customer service manager a position on the company's blog management team.

• *Training Professional.* Your organization's rules and policies are only as good as your employees' willingness to adhere to them. Spend at least as much time communicating your blog rules and policy as you do developing them.

All bloggers, regardless of rank or title, should undergo blog training. If the CEO and other senior executives operate blogs, be sure they have been educated about all the risks, rules, regulations, policies, and procedures associated with blogging.

BLOG RULE #10: Don't allow IT (or legal, records management, or human resources) to dictate your business blog program. Work as a team to implement rules, policies, and procedures based on the best practices detailed in *Blog Rules*.

2. Establish Your Objective First; Blog Second

Just because a blog is easy to establish, inexpensive to operate, and (potentially) effective as a business communications tool, that does not mean a business blog is really right for every organization.

Assign your blog management team the task of establishing a clear objective for your organization's business blog. In other words, why does your organization want to blog? What do you hope to accomplish with your business blog? Does your organization have the type of unique perspective or voice necessary to distinguish your blog from the rest of the pack? What potential positives and negatives can blogging deliver to your organization? Is a blog the right medium to communicate your organization's message? Do you have the time, talent, and focus necessary to operate a successful business blog? Those are just a few of the factors to consider before activating a business blog.

3. Support Blog Policy with Employee Education

The courts tend to respond favorably to written rules and policies, supported by formal employee training that is consistently applied. Train employees about blog risks, rules, rights, and regulations to help ensure compliance with policy. Should your organization ever land on the wrong side of a workplace lawsuit, a formal blog training program may help convince the court that management has done its best to keep the organization free from inappropriate or illegal blog postings and comments.

4. Protect Confidential Data, Trade Secrets, Intellectual Property

Employees may be privy to the confidential information of the organization and its employees, as well as the trade secrets of third parties including business partners, customers, and suppliers. If an employee were to post confidential information on the company's blog or on a personal blog that is hosted by the company's system, the company might be open to legal claims alleging trade secret violation and breach of contract.[2]

Assign the blog management team the task of establishing rules, policies, and procedures to protect trade secrets, confidential information, and private data. Have the team evaluate technology tools that are designed to automatically block employees' access to external blogs, on which they can accidentally (or intentionally) post comments that may expose the organization's trade secrets or otherwise disclose confidential company information.

Require all employees to sign confidentiality agreements in which they agree to keep secrets under wraps and otherwise protect the confidential data of the organization, employees, customers, business partners, and other third parties. Be sure your organization's written confidentiality agreement clearly applies to blog posts and comments that are published by employees on the organization's business blogs, employees' personal blogs, and other external blogs.

Finally, require employees to sign and date an acknowledgment form stating that they have read the confidentiality agreement, understand it, and agree to comply with it or accept the consequences up to and including termination.

> **BLOG RULE #11**: Require employees to sign a confidentiality agreement to protect trade secrets and confidential data belonging to the organization, employees, customers, business partners, and other third parties. Cover blog posts and comments published on the organization's business blogs, employees' personal blogs, and other external blogs, as well.

5. Discipline Blog Policy Violators

According to the Society for Human Resource Management, 3 percent of employers have disciplined employees for blogging.[3] Many organizations—including Microsoft, Starbucks, and Delta Airlines[4] to name just three—have already fired employees for inappropriate blog use. To help maximize employee compliance with blog rules, put some teeth in your organization's policy. Spell out blog content and usage rules in writing, stress the fact that the organization's rules and policies apply regardless of whether employees are blogging at the office or at home on their own time and equipment, and let employees know that any violation of the organization's rules and policies may result in disciplinary action, up to and including termination.

> **BLOG RULE #12**: Use discipline to maximize employee compliance with blog rules, policies, and procedures. Put blog content and usage rules in writing, and stress the fact that the organization's rules and policies apply regardless of whether employees are blogging at the office or at home on their own time and equipment. Inform employees that any violation of the organization's rules and policies may result in disciplinary action, up to and including termination.

6. Note Special Considerations for Public Companies

Unmanaged blog content could land a publicly traded company in hot water with the SEC, exposing the company to liability for violations of federal securities laws. From securities fraud, to jumping the gun, to selective disclosure, to forward-looking statements, public companies must ensure that employee-bloggers do not post untrue content, disclose insider information, or otherwise violate securities laws.[5]

7. Follow HIPAA Regulations

Companies in the health care industry are legally required by the Health Insurance Portability and Accountability Act (HIPAA) to protect the privacy of patient information. HIPAA requires health care organizations to safeguard electronic documents (including blogs) that contain protected health information (PHI) related to a patient's health status, medical care, treatment plans, and payment issues. Failure to do so can result in expensive regulatory fines, civil litigation, criminal charges, and jail time. Use policy, training, and technology to ensure the safe and compliant use of blogs to communicate HIPAA-regulated patient information, or suffer potentially stiff penalties for noncompliance.

8. Address Readers' Comments

If you ask for comments, people will comment. Blogging "culture" is not necessarily polite, but it is honest.[6] If a reader takes time to post a comment or send an e-mail in response to a blog post, be responsive and gracious. You are not required to publish every comment that comes your way (particularly if a third-party's comment is untruthful, unkind, or otherwise likely to create legal problems or other concerns for the organization). However, you are obligated to treat every reader and every correspondent with professional courtesy.

9. Review Pre-Post Content

Given the risks inherent in business blogging, employers are advised to screen writers' posts and readers' comments pre-post to avoid publishing content that is defamatory or inaccurate, violates copyright law, reveals confidential information, or is otherwise inappropriate, offensive, or in violation of rules, regulations, and policies. Prescreen content manually or automatically with content management and aggregation tools. Reject any posts or comments that fail to pass the "smell test."

10. Retain Blog Business Records

Just like e-mail and instant messages, blog posts and readers' comments can create electronic business records. In light of the fact that organizations are increasingly relying on blogs to engage in two-way conversations with both internal and external audiences, it's a safe bet that many business blogs are treasure troves of electronic business records.

If your employees are blogging about your company, its products, services, transactions, suppliers, customers, executives, and staff, then chances are they are creating electronic business records that the organization is obligated to save, store, and (in the event of a lawsuit) hand over to litigators.

11. Respond to What Bloggers Write About You— Good or Bad

The blogosphere is all about transparency, trust, and relationships. If a reader writes something negative about your organization, products, or posts, respond to the comment. If you don't, it will look as though you have something to hide.

If another blogger publishes a particularly negative product review or nasty comment about your organization, consider countering with your own even-handed, factual response plus a link to your critic's blog. If you are a well-known, high-profile company that bloggers are writing about, you can be certain that others will link to the negative post, even if you don't. In the interest of damage control, strive to be the first blogger out of the box with a reply and a link—any time a positive or negative post about your organization appears.

If you discover that factual inaccuracies or misrepresentations about your organization are circulating in the blogosphere via readers' comments and bloggers' posts, that's the time to put your own *blog mob* to work. Use your organization's blog, your employees' business and personal blogs, and the blogs of customer evangelists, and brand bloggers (see Chapter 19) to set the record straight and make the facts known. Your goal is to sway opinion, not ignite an argument. So state your fact-based position even-handedly and respectfully.

In the event that a blogger has defamed your organization or an employee, first ask the blogger to remove the defamatory post. If that tactic fails, contact your lawyer.

12. Monitor the Blogosphere

Keep track of what is being written about your organization in the blogosphere. Subscribe to blog search engines like Google News Alerts (www

.google.com/alerts), PubSub (www.pubsub.com), DayPop (www.daypop
.com), Technorati (www.technorati.com), Feedster (www.feedster.com),
IceRocket (www.icerocket.com), or BlogPulse (www.blogpulse.com) to
find out just what bloggers have to say—about your organization, executives, products, blogs, competitors, and just about any topic you can think
of. Monitoring is also the best way to determine if your blog content has
been stolen by sploggers (spam bloggers).

Recap and Blog Action Plan

1. Form a comprehensive blog risk-management, compliance, and
   litigation response team to determine whether a business blog program is right for your company; to evaluate the risks facing your
   organization and industry should you opt to blog; to establish blog
   rules and policy that meet the organization's legal, regulatory, security, technology, and management needs; and to coordinate the
   blog policy with human resources, public relations, records management, IT, and employee training needs.
2. Assign a blog czar to oversee the organization's blog risk management program and communicate to all employees the fact that
   management takes the business blog program—and compliance
   with the organization's blog rules and policy—seriously.
3. Assign your blog management team the task of establishing a clear
   objective for your organization's business blog. Do not enter the
   blogosphere unless your organization has the focus and perspective, time, and talent necessary to make a business blog succeed.
4. Training employees about blog risks, rules, rights, and regulations
   will help ensure compliance with policy.
5. Require employees to sign a confidentiality agreement to protect
   the trade secrets and confidential data of the organization, employees, customers, partners, and other third parties.
6. Use discipline to maximize employee compliance with blog rules
   and policy, regardless of whether employees are blogging at the
   office or at home on their own time and equipment.

PART 2

LEGAL RISKS AND REGULATORY RULES IN THE BLOGOSPHERE

Why Every Employer Must Establish Blog Policies and Procedures

CHAPTER 5

TREAT BLOG POSTS AS BUSINESS RECORDS

Our legal department loves the blogs, because it basically is a written-down, backed-up, permanent time-stamped version of the scientist's notebook. When you want to file a patent, you can now show in blogs where this idea happened.

—MARISSA MAYER, GOOGLE, QUOTED IN *FORTUNE*[1]

If employees are blogging about your company, its products, services, transactions, suppliers, customers, executives, and staff, then chances are they are creating electronic business records that the organization is obligated to save, store, and (in the event of a lawsuit) hand over to litigators. If your employee-bloggers are corresponding with their readers via e-mail, then they may be creating even more business records that must be retained and archived. If your organization allows readers to post comments on business blogs, then another potential cache of electronic business records is being compiled.

BLOG RULE #13: Treat blog posts and comments as business records that must be retained, archived, and readily available to courts or regulators in the event of a workplace lawsuit or regulatory investigation.

What Is a Blog Business Record?

Not every blog post or comment creates a business record. A business record—whether published on a blog or otherwise produced—is a document that provides evidence of business-related activities, events, transactions, negotiations, purchases, sales, hirings, firings, and so on.[2] Purely personal blog posts about non–business-related matters are unlikely to create business records.

An employee who uses a company blog to display photos of a new puppy or chronicle a family vacation probably is not creating business records that need to be retained. However, if employees blog about the organization, its employees, products, services, suppliers, operations, customers, hiring practices, transactions, or any other business-related matter, then they are creating electronic business records. These need to be retained, archived, and made readily available to lawyers or auditors in the event of litigation or a regulatory investigation.

There Is No Universal Definition of Business Record

Because there is no standard, one-size-fits-all definition of *business record,* every organization must establish its own clear, comprehensive, and consistently enforced definition to protect its business, regulatory, and legal interests. Some organizations opt to establish one companywide definition. Other organizations define *business record* on a department-by-department basis. An organization would require more than one definition of business record if, for example, some employees performed regulated job functions and others did not. The employees who perform tasks that are controlled by government or industry regulations would need to manage blog content and record retention in accordance with regulatory guidelines, as well as the organization's own rules, policies, and procedures.

Litigators and Regulators Demand the Retention of Blog Business Records

If you are struggling with the retention of blog business records (and perhaps e-mail and IM business records, as well), you are not alone. Business owners, executives, IT professionals, and records managers are often confused about electronic business record retention. Even the courts' federal and state rule advisory committees are struggling to assess and as necessary revise rules governing what electronic data are discoverable, how that information should be produced, and which litigants should bear the costs of producing electronic evidence.[3]

In the face of all that confusion, these facts are clear: Using electronic business records as evidence is standard operating procedure in U.S. courtrooms. For more than 30 years, since 1970, electronic data (including the history of employees' Internet surfing, intranet postings, e-mail messages, IM chat, and now blog entries and comments) have been recognized as evidence in federal court.[4]

One in five U.S. companies (20 percent) has had employee e-mail subpoenaed in the course of a workplace lawsuit or regulatory investigation, according to the 2004 Workplace E-Mail and Instant Messaging Survey from American Management Association and The ePolicy Institute. And another 13 percent of organizations have gone to court to battle lawsuits triggered by employee e-mail.[5] Blogs, which are more content-rich and decidedly more permanent than e-mail, are certain to play an equally significant evidentiary role in employment-related litigation as more and more organizations adopt business blogs for use as internal and external communications tools.

A Business Record Is a Business Record

The courts and regulators make absolutely no distinction between electronic business records, such as blog posts and e-mail messages, and traditional paper records, such as handwritten notes on appointment calendars and printed documents stored in metal filing cabinets.

A business record is a business record, regardless of the technology that is used to create it. Business records are judged on the value of their content (what they say), not the type of technology that is used to create them.

All organizations—regardless of the industry in which they operate, the number of workers they employ, their status as public or private entities, or their position as regulated or unregulated businesses—have an obligation to save and store blog business records for legal, regulatory, and business management purposes.

In the event of a workplace lawsuit, blog posts may contain evidence that will be sought by either your own legal team or the opposing legal counsel. Your organization's decision to retain and archive blog business records—and your subsequent ability (or inability) to produce subpoenaed documents in their entirety and within the time limits imposed by the legal system—will be carefully and critically scrutinized by the court.

You Cannot Hide Behind Technology

The courts and regulators have repeatedly demonstrated an expectation that litigators can and will apply technology solutions to the workplace problems that are created by technology. In other words, if your computer system can facilitate blogging, it should be able to capture and store blog business records. During *discovery*—the process by which information and evidence (including blog posts) are collected and exchanged to help lawyers on both sides of a case prepare for trial—your organization cannot hide behind technology. You cannot claim that its computer system is too old or inadequate to allow for effective document response. Nor can you claim that it will take too long or cost too much to produce blog business records or other electronic evidence.[6]

The courts have traditionally ruled that searching e-mail messages is a crucial part of discovery, a process that does not pose an undue burden of time, technology, or cost on an organization that is involved in litigation. It is reasonable to assume that the courts will adopt a similar attitude toward the production of blog business records.[7] Expect to produce subpoenaed blog records and other electronic documents or face the consequences: Court sanctions range from the imposition of monetary fines, to instructions that negatively influence juries, to decisions to quickly settle what now may be a no-win case.

Still Don't Retain E-Mail? Then You're Not Ready to Blog

In light of heightened regulatory oversight and the United States' highly litigious corporate culture, the business community's failure to retain and archive electronic business records according to formal, written retention policies is alarming. Only 35 percent of employers have an e-mail retention policy in place, according to American Management Association/ePolicy Institute research.[8]

Where does your organization stand when it comes to the retention and archiving of e-mail business records and the deletion of nonessential messages? Does your organization have in place a written e-mail retention and deletion policy that is supported by comprehensive employee training and up-to-date technology tools? If not, you are not ready to blog.

Use the establishment of your organization's blog management program as an opportunity to review all electronic communications policies. Update (or create) e-mail, instant message, Internet, intranet, and blog policies based on the best practices detailed in *Blog Rules*. Be sure your organization's written rules and policies address content, confidentiality, copyright, personal usage, and business record retention, among other key issues.

> **BLOG RULE #14:** Use the establishment of your blog program as an opportunity to review all electronic communications policies. Update (or create) e-mail, instant message, Internet, intranet, and blog policies based on best practices detailed in *Blog Rules*.

Failure to Produce Electronic Business Records Cost One Company $1.45 Billion!

Need proof that the legal system takes electronic business-record retention seriously? Courts in recent years have imposed million-dollar sanctions and juries have awarded billion-dollar verdicts against companies that have failed to properly manage, retain, and produce e-mail business records. There is no reason to assume that the same fate does not await organizations that shirk their responsibilities to properly save, systematically store, and promptly produce complete and trustworthy blog business records.

Consider these recent seven- and ten-figure e-mail retention disaster stories:

- Partly in response to Morgan Stanley's failure to preserve and turn over subpoenaed e-mail messages and attachments to the court, a jury in 2005 awarded $1.45 billion in damages against Morgan Stanley.[9]
- A court's instruction to a jury to draw an adverse inference about UBS Warburg for its failure to preserve e-mail evidence resulted in a $29.3 million verdict for ex-employee Laura Zubulake in her widely publicized employment discrimination trial in 2005.[10]
- A federal court in 2004 sanctioned Philip Morris $2.75 million for failing to retain senior executives' e-mail messages over a two-year period. The company was fined for its spoliation, or destruction, of e-mail evidence.[11]

Could your organization survive a million-dollar verdict or a billion-dollar jury award—on top of the six- or seven-figure professional fees charged by your legal defense team? Even if your organization has the financial wherewithal to weather a blog-related legal disaster, the publicity surrounding high-profile litigation could do irreparable damage to your corporate reputation and standing among customers, investors, prospective employees, the media, government officials, and other target audiences—

the same group of influencers (ironically) that you are trying to affect positively via your corporate blog.

Establish a Litigation Response Team and Plan

If you don't yet have a strategic litigation response plan in place to guide you step by step through the discovery process, you are not alone. Eighty-three percent of litigators surveyed by the American Bar Association in 2000 reported that their clients had not yet established procedures for handling electronic discovery requests.[12]

Prepare today for the likelihood that you will be asked to produce blog business records tomorrow. As part of your comprehensive blog management program, assign your legal counsel, compliance officer, records manager, chief technology officer, and human resources director to your organization's litigation response team. Make the litigation response team responsible for enforcing written rules and policies governing employees' blog use and content, establishing electronic data retention policies, ensuring that the organization's electronic data destruction procedures halt as soon as you become aware that a lawsuit is in play or at risk of being filed, and delivering exactly what the court wants—in exactly the form the court wants it—in response to discovery requests involving blog posts or any other electronic documents.[13]

Employers Fail to Educate Employees About Business Records

Fully 63 percent of employees admit that they do not know the difference between an electronic business record that must be retained and an insignificant, purely personal nonrecord that may be deleted. In spite of that knowledge gap, only 27 percent of employers devote time and resources to formally educate employees about business record retention.[14]

Training is integral to compliance. As part of your organization's overall blog management program, be sure to provide employees with a clear definition of *business record* in the context of your company, its various departments, and industry. Establish clear, consistent, written electronic business-record retention rules and policies for blogs, e-mail, instant messager, the Internet, the intranet, and other electronic communications tools. Then educate all employee-bloggers, including the CEO and other senior executives, about the organization's comprehensive electronic business record definition(s), policies, and procedures.

> **BLOG RULE #15**: Employee training is key to compliance with blog content and usage rules and retention policy.

Combine Rules with Technology to Help Manage Blog Business Records

Although blog technology has yet to catch up with usage, be sure to take advantage of the technology tools that currently exist to help organizations manage their blog risks. Content management tools, such as iUpload's blogging platform, enable organizations to preview, edit, aggregate, and otherwise manage employee postings. Content security solutions, such as St. Bernard's iPrism appliance or Clearswift's MIMEsweeper, enable management to block and filter employees' access to external blogs that reside outside the organization's firewall. Blog search engines allow organizations to search the blogosphere automatically to see what is being written about the company by employees, customers, competitors, and the blogosphere in general.

Although technology has yet to be developed specifically to retain and archive blog business records, that does not release your organization from its obligation to do so. Rely on the expertise of your chief technology officer, legal counsel, and records manager to determine the most effective approach to blog retention and archiving. Your goal is to retain business records in a manner that ensures their trustworthiness, authenticity, completeness, and integrity. The courts and regulators should have no trouble accepting them as reliable evidence.

A few retention options: (1) consider using the same technology your organization uses to capture and archive Web content; (2) if your organization uses an enterprise content management system to control, capture, and archive e-mail and IM business records, it may work with blogs, too; (3) consider using an enterprise-grade blog publishing platform like iUpload's product, which retains every version of every post and archives content for easy retrieval;[15] (4) if all else fails, print out and systematically file every business-related blog post and comment.

How Long Should You Keep Blog Business Records?

Unless your organization's blog content is governed by law or regulation—such as the SEC's dictate that brokerage firms be prepared to produce three years' worth of electronic records immediately upon request, or the Employee Retirement Income Security Act's rule that e-mail and other documents related to employee benefit plans be kept indefinitely[16]—you are free to determine the retention period that is right for your organization. As a rule, you should keep electronic business records (including blog posts and comments) for the same length of time as paper records. Consistency is key.[17] As electronic business records play a growing evidentiary role in litigation, the trend among many employers is to hold on to e-mail messages, IM chat, blog posts and comments, and other electronic business records for increasingly longer periods of time.

Recap and Blog Action Plan

1. Treat blog posts and readers' comments as electronic business records that must be retained, archived, and readily available to courts or regulators in the event of a workplace lawsuit or regulatory investigation.

2. Define the meaning of *business record* for your organization. If necessary, define the term on a department-by-department basis.

3. Create a formal, written, blog business-record retention policy. At the same time, review your retention rules and policies for e-mail, instant messaging, the Internet, intranet, and other electronic data. Update or create new rules, policies, and procedures as necessary.

4. Educate employees about electronic business records, including blog records, the organization's blog retention policy, content guidelines, regulatory compliance requirements, and enforcement guidelines.

5. Take advantage of existing technology to support your organization's blog risk-management and retention policies and procedures.

BLOGS CREATE MILLION-DOLLAR (SOMETIMES BILLION-DOLLAR) LEGAL HEADACHES FOR EMPLOYERS

Bloggers are more of a threat than people realize, and they are only going to get more toxic.

—Peter Blackshaw, Intelliseek, quoted in *Forbes*[1]

Blog posts and comments, just like e-mail messages, create the electronic equivalent of DNA evidence. Every time an employee writes a post on your business blog, each time a customer or other third party posts a comment on an employee's blog, any time an employee-blogger and a reader engage in e-mail correspondence, legal evidence for (or against) the organization is created.

Although blog-related litigation is still fairly uncommon, you can count on bloggers' posts and readers' comments playing a growing evidentiary role in workplace lawsuits.

Be Prepared: Anticipate Blog-Related Legal Risks

As detailed in *Law Technology News*, blogging raises the same issues for employers as the publication of written content in other media.[2] In other words, it is the nature of the content (what is written), not the technology that is used (blog software) to produce the content (posts and comments), that counts when it comes to creating business records, evidence, and risks.

Consequently, "employers may be legitimately concerned about the potential for inadvertent or intentional disclosure of confidential information or trade secrets. They may worry that employees will discuss business matters without the knowledge or oversight of management. And they want to prevent the defamation of the company or a 'false light' portrayal."[3]

In addition to worrying about employees' blog posts, employers should be concerned about the potential for disaster when customers and other third parties log on to company blogs and post comments that infringe on copyrights, are defamatory, or otherwise pose risks.

Consider some of the legal risks facing employers who operate business blogs:

- Once you begin accepting commentary from customers and other third parties on your business blog, your organization could be deemed a publisher if you edit the submission. As a publisher, you may be liable for defamation, slander, libel, and other claims triggered by the inappropriate content posted by outsiders in the comment section of your business blog. You can't control what people write—unless you opt to edit comments prior to posting them. If you opt to edit, then you face a twofold problem: (1) as a publisher, your organization may be viewed as part of any problem that may arise; and (2) as an editor, you may be accused of sanitizing your business blog—cleansing it of the freewheeling commentary that helps make a blog a blog.[4]

- An employer could face a *false-light* defamation claim if an employee were to post on the company's blog a doctored image that falsely depicts a third-party engaged in a crime. If injured by the doctored photo, the third-party could potentially file a claim against both the blogger and the blogger's employer.[5]

- If an employee were to intercept an e-mail message or other document, then post it to the organization's blog, the employer might face an invasion of privacy claim. Even if the employee were blogging at home on a personal site, the organization might be held responsible if a reasonable person could assume that the employer was aware of the employee's actions.[6]

- *Vicarious liability* (and the related legal concept of *respondeat superior*) is the legal term that is used when an organization is held responsible for the bad acts of its employees.[7] "The mere tolerance of workplace blogging could be viewed as a corporate endorsement of the blog's content," according to legal experts.[8] In the case of *Blakey v. Continental Airlines, Inc.*, for example, the New Jersey Supreme Court ruled that an employer who was aware that employees were engaging in a pattern of retaliatory harassment while using a work-related online chat room, and failed to stop the harassment, could be held liable.[9] Similarly, "employers may also face potential liability for defamation if a blogger-employee publishes defamatory statements."[10]

"Cybersmear" Lawsuits Receive a Mixed Reception by the Courts

A growing number of companies are filing "cybersmear" claims against bloggers who publish posts (often anonymously) that criticize, attack, or embarrass the organization. To that end, companies increasingly are asking the courts to force Internet service providers to reveal the identities of anonymous bloggers who post defamatory statements. The courts, however, have not been consistent in their rulings when it comes to blog attacks.

For example, in the case *Immunomedics, Inc. v. Doe,* the New Jersey appellate court upheld a subpoena seeking to force Yahoo to reveal the identity of an anonymous blogger who, using the pseudonym "Worried Employee," posted messages detailing problems with the biopharmaceutical company's European operations. The company claimed the blogger's posts revealed confidential company information.[11]

By contrast, in a widely publicized 2005 case, the Delaware Supreme Court ruled that a city official who claimed to have been defamed by an anonymous blogger could not use a lawsuit to unmask the blogger. This marked the first time that a state Supreme Court ruled on the rights of anonymous bloggers.[12]

Compounding the problem is that fact that, given the nature of the blogosphere, it is the victim, not the attacker, who may end up looking bad if a lawsuit is filed. File suit against a blogger, and you are likely to find your cease-and-desist letter posted, your threats of legal action published and ridiculed online, and detailed accounts of depositions and trial proceedings posted for all the blogosphere to read.[13] The fallout, in terms of negative publicity and ill will, may be more damaging than the original blog attack.

Don't Let Your Blog Become a Breeding Ground for Sexual Harassment Claims

With 89 percent of corporations surveyed either blogging now or planning to blog in the future,[14] expect to see blog posts and comments enter into the evidence pool in sexual harassment claims, sexual discrimination cases, and hostile work environment lawsuits. An employee might, for example, allege that a hostile work environment has been created by the unwelcome and persistent sexual conduct of coworkers who are posting off-color or suggestive comments, dirty jokes, or obscene photos on internal company blogs—and in the process creating a hostile work environment for the offended victim.

> **BLOG RULE #16**: Expect to see employees' blog posts and readers' comments enter the evidence pool in sexual harassment claims, discrimination cases, and hostile work environment lawsuits.

The potential cost to defend a sexual harassment claim or hostile work environment lawsuit can be staggering when you factor in legal fees, expert witness fees, discovery costs, court sanctions, and settlement costs. Be proactive. Use your organization's written blog rules and policy to prohibit employees from writing posts that contain sexual innuendos; off-color or dirty jokes; comments about another person's sex life, sexual history, or sexual preference; use of "pet" names; obscene language; or sexual content of any kind, including photos, videos, art, graphics, cartoons, and text.

Remember, business blogs exist primarily for business purposes. Sexually charged content has no place in a business environment or on a business blog. Monitor employees' blogs at the office and at home to ensure that all employees are adhering to the organization's blog content and language guidelines, sexual harassment and discrimination policy, ethics guidelines, and code of conduct.

Noncompliance puts the organization's reputation, assets, and future at risk. When a policy violation occurs, act swiftly to discipline the employee-blogger, delete the offensive content from the organization's blog, and remind all employees that compliance with the organization's written rules and policies is mandatory, not optional.

> **BLOG RULE #17**: Enhance your organization's legal position—and increase the likelihood of successfully defending a sexual harassment or hostile work environment claim someday—by establishing a comprehensive written blog policy and enforcing that policy with a consistent program of training, technology, and discipline.

Reduce Legal Exposures Before Disaster Strikes

Expect inappropriate, unmanaged blog posts to trigger high-profile, high-cost, highly publicized litigation as more companies add blogging to the business communications mix. Put best practices–based policy, training, and technology to work today to prevent the likelihood of your organization becoming the poster child for business-blog litigation tomorrow. The following list lays out a strategy for doing that.

- *Establish written policy.* Effective blog risk management begins with a comprehensive, written blog policy. Address usage, content, language, online etiquette (or "netiquette"), confidentiality, copyright, defamation, business use, personal use, monitoring, discipline, and other important issues. The establishment of your organization's blog policy is a good time to review and, as necessary, update all of the company's employment policies. The company should look at, for example, sexual harassment and discrimination guidelines, ethics rules, electronic-communications policy, confidentiality and nondisclosure agreements, netiquette guidelines, and the employee code of conduct. Make sure employees understand that all of the organization's employment policies apply to blogging. Stress the fact that compliance with all company policies is mandatory.

- *Provide adequate training.* The courts appreciate, and tend to respond favorably to, policy and training consistently applied.[15] Do not leave blog policy compliance to chance. Educate all employee-bloggers about blog-related risks, rules, regulations, rights, responsibilities, policies, and procedures. Require all employees to sign and date an acknowledgment form, confirming that they have participated in formal blog policy training. Keep those acknowledgment forms on file. You may one day need to demonstrate to the court that the organization has done everything possible to ensure blog policy compliance.

- *Conduct a legal review of the blog's content.* Sure, a legal review of posts and comments will slow down the blogging process and dampen spontaneity. What's the alternative? A seven-figure lawsuit and the loss of your organization's good name? Do not take chances with written blog content. Assign a member of the legal team or another responsible individual to review every writer's post and each reader's comment prior to publication.

- *Think twice before letting customers and other third parties post.* If you accept and edit commentary from customers and other third parties on your business blog, your organization could be deemed a publisher. As such, you may be liable for defamation, slander, libel, copyright infringement, and other claims triggered by inappropriate comments posted by outsiders. Either control risks with pre-post editing or do not accept third-party comments.

• *Don't allow employees to post anonymously.* For a disgruntled employee, an anonymous blog may provide a terrific opportunity to vent, rant, whine, and otherwise complain about the people, products, and conditions at your company. Prevent employee gripe sites before they get started. Use the company's blog policy to inform employees that they are prohibited from blogging anonymously about the organization on company-sponsored blogs or their own personal blogs. If the organization is mentioned, the employee must be identified by name, title, and company affiliation.

• *Monitor the blogosphere.* The easiest and most effective way to stay on top of what people (employees, competitors, customers, and others) are writing about your organization is to monitor the blogosphere. Subscribe to blog search engines, and assign someone the task of regularly tracking blogs. Although it may not be legally required in your state, it's a good idea for employers in all 50 states to let employees know that management is monitoring their blog activity—at work and home. For added protection, require employees to sign an acknowledgment form confirming that they are aware that the organization regularly monitors the blogosphere, including employees' business and personal sites, as part of the company's electronic risk-management program.

• *Discipline policy violators.* If monitoring unearths a policy violation, act immediately to discipline the employee-blogger in question. Let one violation slide today, and you may find yourself battling a department full of blog policy scofflaws tomorrow. Use your written policy to spell out the penalties, up to and including termination, that await employees who fail to comply with the organization's blog policy or any other employment policies.

Recap and Blog Action Plan

1. Every time an employee writes a post on your business blog, each time a customer or other third party posts a comment on an employee's blog, any time an employee-blogger and a reader engage in e-mail correspondence, legal evidence for (or against) the organization is created.

2. Employee blog posts and third-party comments can open the organization up to allegations of hostile work environment, sexual harassment, racial discrimination, copyright infringement, trade secret violation, defamation, slander, libel, and invasion of privacy, among other legal claims.

3. To help keep blog content compliant, and to reduce the likelihood of employees' posts and readers' comments triggering legal claims or providing smoking-gun evidence of wrongdoing, employers are advised to put in place a blog policy backed by training, monitoring, and other best practices.

CHAPTER 7

SHHH! BLOGS PUT TRADE SECRETS AND CONFIDENTIAL INFORMATION AT RISK

Picture the blog world as the biggest coffeehouse on Earth.

—*BusinessWeek*[1]

Blogging Compounds Confidentiality Concerns

Even more than e-mail and instant messaging, blogs increase the risk of confidentiality breaches that may be triggered when—caught up in the unstructured, unfiltered, anything-goes culture of the blogosphere— employees (accidentally or intentionally) write and publish posts about confidential, proprietary, or private matters that would be better (and more safely) discussed in a face-to-face meeting behind closed doors.[2]

An employee-blogger could, for example, inadvertently disclose a trade secret that belongs to one of the organization's business partners. That blog post could, in turn, set off a breach of contract suit, a claim alleging the misappropriation of the partner's trade secret, and the termination of the offending employee.[3]

You don't even have to be a blog writer to create confidentiality and trade secret concerns. Blog readers are equally capable of violating privacy, disclosing trade secrets, and divulging insider information when they post comments on others' sites.

What's to stop a disgruntled employee from sitting down at a home computer at the end of the workday, cocktail in hand, and pounding out an angry post in which confidential company information is leaked? Let's not forget vengeful former employees, disgruntled customers, and malicious outsiders who might be delighted to share (anonymously, of course) your organization's trade secrets and intellectual property with the blogosphere.

Compounding the problem is the fact that employees who use free consumer-grade blog software and public hosting services at the office, rather than relying on secure enterprise-grade blog systems, open the organization to data theft and other security breaches, including splog and comment spam attacks.

As if that were not troubling enough, the U.S. Supreme Court, in *Bartnicki v. Vopper*, ruled that people who innocently receive stolen trade secrets via electronic communications tools may have a free-speech right to disclose the information, provided the disclosure involves a matter of public importance.[4]

Secrets Never Die in the Blogosphere

When bloggers reveal confidential information or trade secrets, it is difficult for the organization, legally and practically, to halt the flow of sensitive data into the blogosphere. The organization can remove an offending post from its own site, and—as you become aware of the post's presence elsewhere— ask other bloggers to remove it, too. However, thanks to incoming links, outgoing links, permalinks, and content syndication, a post that contains confidential information can—and quite possibly will—travel to millions of blogs, where it will be read, retained, archived, and accessible to new readers forever.

Digital Millennium Copyright Act Protects Against Copyright Infringement Liability

If your organization allows customers and other outside readers to post comments or ask questions on your business blog—and those users were to accidentally or intentionally post content (text, art, videos, photos, etc.) that is protected by a third-party's copyright—your organization could be held vicariously liable for copyright infringement. To make matters worse, as a third-party copyright infringer, your organization could be subject to treble damages—unless the company has followed the procedures necessary to ensure *safe harbor protection* from liability through the Digital Millennium Copyright Act (DMCA).[5]

An added bonus: According to attorney Doug Isenberg of GigaLaw.com, the DMCA protects the organization even if it has fed copyright-protected content into the blog syndication pipeline, leaving the infringed-upon material in the blogosphere long after an organization has pulled it off a website as the law requires.[6]

Washington, D.C.–based attorney David Snead notes that the DMCA is a "ridiculously easy" preventive measure for any organization that operates a business blog program to adopt—yet few companies have taken advantage of the law's protections.

To qualify for DMCA safe harbor protection from third-party liability for copyright infringement, the organization must follow three steps:

1. Designate a DMCA agent with the Library of Congress.
2. List the organization's designated DMCA agent on the company's website. Also provide a recap of the DMCA-mandated protocols that the organization follows when responding to allegations of third-party copyright infringement.
3. Design and implement an internal compliance plan based on the DMCA's requirements for handling complaints.[7]

Be sure to have your legal counsel review all DMCA policies, procedures, and requirements to ensure that your organization has done everything necessary—registered a designated DMCA agent, completed all the necessary paperwork, adhered to all the required procedures—to ensure compliance and safe harbor protection. Do not solicit or post comments by customers or other blog readers until the DMCA registration process is complete.

A note of caution: Legal experts warn that DMCA safe harbor protections may not apply if an employee were to post infringing information on the organization's blog. This issue has not yet been tested by case law.[8] Until it is, use policy and training to ensure that employees understand copyright law and comply fully with the organization's rules and policies regarding copyright infringement.

BLOG RULE #18: As a third-party copyright infringer (thanks to customers' blog comments) the organization could be subject to treble damages. Seek safe-harbor protection from liability through the Digital Millennium Copyright Act (DMCA).

Recap and Blog Action Plan

1. Even more than e-mail and instant messaging, blogs increase the risk of confidentiality breaches that may be triggered when em-

ployees publish posts about confidential, proprietary, or private matters.

2. Blog readers are capable of violating privacy, disclosing trade secrets, and divulging insider information when they post comments on others' sites.

3. When bloggers reveal confidential information or trade secrets, it is difficult for the organization, legally and practically, to halt the flow of sensitive data into the blogosphere. Thanks to links and syndication, a post that contains confidential information can remain in the blogosphere forever.

4. As a third-party copyright infringer (thanks to readers' comments), the organization could be subject to treble damages. Seek safe-harbor protection from liability through the Digital Millennium Copyright Act (DMCA).

CHAPTER 8

BLOG BEST PRACTICES FOR PUBLIC COMPANIES AND REGULATED FIRMS

Web logs are the prized platform of an online lynch mob spouting liberty but spewing lies, libel, and invective.

—*FORBES*[1]

Unmanaged blog content could land a publicly traded company in hot water with the Securities and Exchange Commission (SEC), exposing the company to liability for violations of federal securities laws. From securities fraud to jumping the gun, selective disclosure, and forward-looking statements, public companies must ensure that employee-bloggers do not post untrue content, disclose insider information, or otherwise violate securities laws.[2]

For public companies and regulated firms, it is particularly important that blog usage and content are managed and controlled, that posts and comments are reviewed by legal or compliance experts before publication, that the organization and its employees maintain strict compliance with government and industry regulatory rules, and that blog business records are retained, archived, and readily accessible in the event of a regulatory audit.

Maximize Compliance with an Anti-Blog Policy

Public companies and regulated firms are concerned enough about security breaches, privacy violations, and other blog-related risks that some have imposed strict anti-blog policies and installed technology to enforce their no-blogging rules. The financial services industry, for example, has largely adopted an anti-blog stance.[3]

Anti-blog policies typically forbid all in-office blogging and prohibit employees from writing about the company or any business-related matter on their personal blogs. Anti-blog policy is supported by content security technology tools, which are used to block employees' access to blogs outside the company firewall, so employees cannot access or post comments on third parties' blogs. Fortunately for these organizations, the technology to filter out blogs is fairly commonplace. "From installing simple URL filters and content scanners to blacklisting ranges of IP addresses, myriad methods for shutting out blog content are available."[4]

A strict anti-blog policy helps publicly traded companies, banks, financial services firms, and other regulated businesses ensure employee compliance with the government and industry rules governing the use of electronic communications tools. Strict compliance, via policy and technology, limits the likelihood that an organization will suffer multimillion-dollar fines or other penalties for employees' blog-related content, usage, and retention violations.

> **BLOG RULE #19**: A strict anti-blog policy, backed by content security technology, helps publicly traded companies and regulated firms ensure employee compliance with regulators' blog-related content, usage, and retention rules.

Regulated Employers Can't Afford to Approach Blog Content and Record Retention as Hit-or-Miss Propositions

For financial services firms, health care organizations, and others in regulated industries, the failure to manage blog content and retain blog business records (both writers' posts and readers' comments) according to regulatory guidelines can (as it regularly has with e-mail and other electronic business records) lead to multimillion-dollar regulatory fines, criminal charges, civil lawsuits, damaged reputations, panicked investors, and searing negative publicity.

Consider two recent examples from the financial services world. JPMorgan paid $2.1 million in 2005 to settle an e-mail retention dispute with the Securities and Exchange Commission (SEC), New York Stock

Exchange (NYSE), and National Association of Securities Dealers (NASD).[5] State Street Research Investment Services paid a $1 million fine to NASD in 2004 to settle investigations into the firm's e-mail retention policies.[6]

If you are unsure which government or industry regulations govern your business and its blogging program, now is the time to find out. Assign a team of legal, compliance, records management, and IT professionals to determine where blogs fit into your organization's regulatory puzzle, and how a program that combines written policy, employee education, and content-management technology can help maximize compliance and minimize blog-related regulatory risks and other disasters.

Regulatory Compliance Necessitates the Protection of Confidential, Nonpublic Information

In addition to retaining, archiving, and someday producing blog posts and other electronic business records, regulated companies are obligated to protect confidential company information and customers' personal nonpublic information.

Whether the organization is a financial services firm regulated by the NYSE, NASD, SEC, and the Gramm-Leach-Bliley Act (GLBA); a public company governed by the Sarbanes-Oxley Act (SOX); a health care provider that must comply with the Health Insurance Portability and Accountability Act (HIPAA); or another type of organization that is regulated by one of the more than 10,000 federal, state, and local regulations in existence today,[7] regulated companies must keep private information safe.

Since most organizations' confidential information is maintained and transmitted electronically, regulatory compliance hinges on your company's ability to effectively manage blog security, usage, and compliance. A confidential, internal blog post can be damaging if it gets exposed to outside readers. If a blogger's e-mail is intercepted or accessed by an intruder, your company is at risk for unauthorized disclosure and other risks.

Don't Let SOX Put Your Organization in a Box

For public companies and registered public accounting firms, inadequate blog management can lead to Sarbanes-Oxley Act (SOX) violations. Intended to allow the Securities and Exchange Commission (SEC) to thwart fraud in public companies, SOX requires regulated companies to implement internal controls for gathering, processing, and reporting accurate and reliable financial information.

In other words, SOX requires businesses to demonstrate effective corporate governance and information management controls. Consequently, blog content or security breaches—from intercepted e-mail messages posted on blogs, to leaked or stolen data shared on a blog—can put an organization at risk of noncompliance.

Just how tough is the SEC on SOX violators? Failure to retain records related to audit work papers and financial controls as mandated by SOX can put an organization at risk of severe penalties for noncompliance. Knowingly altering or destroying records that are vital to an audit or investigation can net guilty parties federal prison terms. Although SOX is vague about electronic requirements and electronic record keeping, employers are advised to implement a blog management program that addresses blog usage, content, security, retention, and archiving as part of the organization's comprehensive SOX compliance plan.

To help avoid SOX violations, it would be prudent to have legal counsel review posts before they are published. Not only will a pre-post legal review help ensure that blog content is clean and compliant, but, as attorney Stephen Fronk of Howard Rice Nemerovski Canady Falk & Rabkin suggests, it also may cast the organization in a better light legally, should the SEC opt to prosecute the company for SOX violations.[8]

Observe the Health Insurance Portability and Accountability Act (HIPAA)

Companies in the health care industry are legally required by HIPAA to protect the privacy of patient information. HIPAA requires health care organizations to safeguard electronic documents (including blog posts) that contain protected health information (PHI) related to a patient's health status, medical care, treatment plans, and payment issues. Failure to do so can result in expensive regulatory fines, civil litigation, criminal charges, and jail time. Organizations that are governed by HIPAA have a choice: either use policy, training, and technology—including blog content management tools—to ensure the safe and compliant use of blogs to communicate HIPAA-regulated patient information, or suffer potentially stiff penalties for noncompliance.

Comply with the Gramm-Leach-Bliley Act (GLBA)

GLBA is to the financial industry what HIPAA is to the health care arena. Under GLBA, financial institutions are legally obligated to protect the privacy of customers and their nonpublic personal information. In spite of Congress's attempts to protect customer privacy and regulate corporate accountability, many organizations remain challenged by GLBA, along with other federal and state regulations. According to a 2003 survey conducted by Harris Interactive Research, fully 85 percent of employees and managers with access to sensitive customer data are unaware of GLBA's mandates to protect consumer data or face fines and jail time.[9]

Employee education is key to regulatory compliance. A company cannot expect untrained employees to be familiar with rules and regulations, appreciate the importance of compliance, or understand their individual roles in the compliance process. Support written blog policy with formal training and stress the fact that regulatory compliance is mandatory.

Follow SEC, NASD, and NYSE Rules and Regulations

Any company regulated by the SEC, NASD, or NYSE that has yet to adopt blog best practices based on regulatory rules should be prepared for robust penalties. Blog syndication poses particular risks for broker-dealers and other regulated firms, when noncompliant copy is linked from site A to site B, where it cannot be retrieved. Employers should assume that the SEC would view blog links, permalinks, and syndication as similarly risky—and therefore would expect regulated companies to act accordingly.

Enforce Language Guidelines to Limit Legal Claims and Regulatory Concerns

One of the most effective ways to reduce blog risk is to control blog content. Appropriate blog posts should comply with regulatory guidelines governing what employees may say to whom. Financial services firms, for example, face protracted and potentially costly regulatory investigations triggered by employees sharing content with members of off-limits departments in violation of SEC guidelines.

Minimize the likelihood of regulatory noncompliance by combining clear and comprehensive content and usage rules with a personal use policy and employee education. Make sure employees understand that blog rules and policies apply—regardless of whether employees are blogging at the office on a company-sponsored blog or at home on their own personal blogs.

Educate Regulated Employees About Risks and Rules

Fully 43 percent of regulated employees either do not adhere to regulatory requirements governing e-mail retention or are unsure if they are in compliance, according to American Management Association and The ePolicy Institute.[10] Only 29 percent of regulated companies believe they have a legal requirement to retain e-mail for a minimum period, reveals Osterman Research.[11] If so many regulated companies and employees are still struggling to comply with e-mail retention rules, what's the likelihood that blog posts and comments will be properly saved and stored?

What steps has your organization taken to ensure that regulated employees are in compliance? If your organization employs individuals who are governed by industry or government regulations, be sure those regulated employees know, understand, and comply with all regulatory rules governing electronic (including blog) content, usage, and retention.

Apply Technology Solutions to Control Usage and Maximize Compliance

Whether a health care worker accidentally posts patients' confidential medical records on a facing-out blog in violation of HIPAA, a disgruntled bank employee turns splogger to steal customers' social security and credit card numbers in violation of GLBA, an untrained employee deletes blog business records that may one day be subpoenaed as evidence, or a vengeful ex-employee posts an embarrassing internal memo on a widely read and linked to external blog—the employer may be held responsible (by regulators and the courts) for the misconduct of employee-bloggers.

Don't leave employee compliance and your organization's future to chance. Combine written blog rules and policy with employee education and policy-based content management technology tools to help minimize potential risks and maximize compliance with regulatory and organizational rules and policy.

Recap and Blog Action Plan

1. The failure to manage blog content and business records according to regulatory guidelines can (as it regularly has with e-mail and other electronic business records) lead to million-dollar fines,

criminal charges, civil lawsuits, damaged reputations, panicked investors, and searing negative publicity.

2. If you are unsure which government or industry regulations govern your company and employee-bloggers, now is the time to find out.

3. Combine written blog rules and policy, employee education, and enterprise-grade content management and security technology to ensure that confidential company information and customers' personal nonpublic information remain secret and secure.

4. Impose strict anti-blog policies, supported by content security technology, to minimize risks and maximize compliance.

PART 3

DESIGNING AND IMPLEMENTING EFFECTIVE BLOG RULES AND POLICIES

USE WRITTEN BLOG RULES AND POLICY TO CONTROL CONTENT, MAXIMIZE COMPLIANCE, AND REDUCE LIABILITIES

Free Expression Can Be Costly When Bloggers Bad-Mouth Jobs.

— *Washington Post*[1]

Regardless of whether your organization opts to operate blogs internally (for employees' eyes only) or externally (for customers and the world to read), it is essential that it establishes written blog rules and policies to support and enforce its strategic blog management program.

When it comes to employee blog use, there simply is no way to guarantee a completely risk-free environment. Whether blogging at the office or at home, even the most conscientious employees are prone to accidents and missteps. And there is always a chance that a rogue employee will intentionally publish blog content that creates legal, regulatory, security, or other problems for the organization.

That said, organizations can limit liability somewhat by developing and implementing comprehensive blog rules and policies that address issues including content, language, confidentiality, copyright, defamation, privacy, monitoring, compliance, personal use, retention, regulatory rules, and disciplinary action, among other key issues.

Blog policies may not be required by law, but they certainly can help keep an organization out of legal hot water. To date, employers have spent millions of dollars defending and settling lawsuits related to the improper use of e-mail, IM, and the Internet. Blogging is certain to make an already litigious business environment even more litigious.

Put Blog Best Practices to Work with the Three Es of Blog Risk Management

Employers who are committed to complying with government regulations, preventing accidental misuse and intentional abuse, and reducing the risk of litigation and other blog-related disasters are advised to put best practices to work by focusing on the *three Es of blog risk management:*

1. Establish policy.
2. Educate employees.
3. Enforce policy with discipline, coupled with blog content management and monitoring technology.

Establish Policy

Establish comprehensive, clearly written blog rules, policies, and procedures to govern employees' business and personal blog usage, content, and retention. Develop written blog policies with regulatory compliance, litigation concerns, security challenges, productivity issues, and overall business needs clearly in mind. Assign your blog management team the task of ensuring that your company's blog policy addresses all the risks, rules, and regulations facing your business and industry.

Blog policies should be clearly written and easy for employees to access, understand, and adhere to. Avoid vague language that may leave the organization's blog policy open to individual employee interpretation. Update written blog policies annually to ensure that your organization has rules, policies, and procedures in place to maximize compliance with any new regulations, laws, or risks that may arise.

Distribute a hard copy of the organization's written blog policy to all employee-bloggers, including the CEO and other senior executives who may be blogging. Insist that all employees sign and date a hard copy of the policy, acknowledging that they have read the policy, understand it, and agree to comply with all the organization's blog-related rules and policies or accept disciplinary action up to and including termination.

Remember, employers are responsible for maintaining a lawful and compliant business environment that is harassment-free, discrimination-free, crime-free, and based on civil business behavior. Developing, implementing, and enforcing a comprehensive blog policy are steps toward accomplishing that goal.

Educate Employees

Support written blog rules and policies with companywide employee training conducted on-site by an in-person trainer or via online webinar or
video. If your organization's CEO or members of senior management are
blogging, be sure they participate in blog risks and rules training, too. Make
sure employees understand that blog policy compliance is mandatory, not
optional. Thanks to blog policy training, employees will better understand
the risks, rules, and responsibilities of blogging. Consequently, employee-
bloggers will be more likely to comply with policy, and the courts may be
more accepting of the fact that your organization has made a reasonable
effort to remain free from discrimination, harassment, hostility, and other
objectionable behavior.

Based on the legal principle known as vicarious liability, an employer
may be held responsible for the accidental or intentional misconduct of
employees. That should serve as a wake-up call to employers who do not
educate employees about e-mail risks, rules, and regulations, much less
blogging.

The courts tend to look favorably on organizations that establish written policies supported by formal training that addresses risks, rules, regulations, and responsibilities. A strategic blog policy and formal employee
training program may one day help your organization defend itself against a
sexual harassment claim, hostile work environment lawsuit, or other blog-
related litigation.

Enforce Policy

Enforce your organization's written blog rules and policies with a combination of disciplinary action, content management tools, and monitoring
technology. If you have any doubt about your employees' willingness to
adhere to the organization's blog usage and content rules, consider applying
a technological solution to what essentially is a people problem. Consider
utilizing a blog content management tool to review and aggregate employee posts, block banned or inappropriate content, and stay on top of
employees' overall blogging activity.

Be sure to take advantage of technology tools that automatically monitor the blogosphere, including employees' business and personal blogs.
Subscribe to blog search engines such as Google News Alerts (www.goo
gle.com/alerts), PubSub (www.pubsub.com), DayPop (www.daypop
.com), Technorati (www.technorati.com), Feedster (www.feedster.com),
IceRocket (www.icerocket.com), or BlogPulse (www.blogpulse.com) to

find out just what your employee-bloggers have to say about your organization, executives, products, trade secrets, business partners, suppliers, blog program, competitors, and just about any other topic.

If monitoring reveals that an employee is violating the organization's blog policy, then it is essential for management to take immediate disciplinary action. Consistently apply discipline to show employees that management is serious about blog policy compliance. Failure to discipline one employee for blog-related misconduct may encourage other employees to violate the organization's written rules and policies and could create liability concerns for the organization.

Employers are getting tougher about electronic policy compliance, with 25 percent reporting that they have fired employees for misusing the organization's e-mail system, and another 26 percent terminating employees for Internet policy violations, according to the 2005 Electronic Monitoring and Surveillance Survey from American Management Association and The ePolicy Institute.[2] Although the Society for Human Resource Management reports that only 3 percent of employers have disciplined employees for blogging,[3] that number is certain to grow as workplace blogging becomes more prevalent.

Blog Policy Best Practices

Consider incorporating the following 12 best practices into your organization's blog policy program to help maximize employee compliance while minimizing organizational risk.

Best Practices for Maximizing Compliance and Minimizing Risk

1. Establish a written policy governing your organization's business blogs.
2. Establish a policy governing employees' personal blog use.
3. Guard professional (and personal) secrets.
4. Prohibit anonymous blogging.
5. Instruct bloggers to use a legal disclaimer.
6. Inform bloggers how to handle media inquiries.
7. Impose financial rules.
8. Require bloggers to keep retention policy in mind.
9. Instruct employees how to handle comment spam and splog.
10. Be sure to notify employees of your corporate blog policy.

11. Use technology to help manage your people problems.
12. Require employees to formally acknowledge blog rules and policy.

Establish a Written Policy Governing Your Organization's Business Blogs

If you operate internal or external blogs on which employees are free to post commentary (business and/or personal), then you must establish and enforce clear rules governing language, content, and usage.

Use your written policy to make sure employees know what type of language and content are allowed and what is banned from the organization's blogs. Twenty-three percent of organizations have policies in place governing the publication of personal posts on corporate blogs.[4] Decide how you are going to handle the issue of business versus personal posts, and let employees know what the rules are.

Remind employees that blog content must be in compliance with the organization's harassment and discrimination policies, confidentiality agreements, ethics rules, code of conduct, and other employment policies. To help prevent smoking-gun blog content from triggering a workplace lawsuit, stock slide, regulatory investigation, or media feeding frenzy, prohibit employees from posting critical opinions or defamatory comments about the organization, its products, services, employees, executives, competitors, partners, suppliers, customers—or anyone else, for that matter.

Establish Policy Governing Employees' Personal Blog Use

Make sure employees understand that all of the organization's written rules and policies apply, regardless of whether employees are operating business blogs from their cubicles at work or personal blogs from their bedrooms at home.

If you allow personal blogging on office computers, notify employees that the computer system is the property of the company, and employees have no reasonable expectation of privacy when using it to operate a personal blog. Also consider setting limits on the amount of time employees may devote to personal, non–business-related blogging. According to American Management Association/ePolicy Institute research, 20 percent of organizations already have implemented policies governing employees' personal blogging on company time.[5]

Instruct employees who operate personal non–business-related blogs outside the office that they are prohibited from discussing the organization, employees, clients, business partners, suppliers, or other third parties associated with the organization; posting company-related content; using the organization's logo, trademarks, advertising slogans, and other copyright-protected material; or otherwise violating the organization's blog rules and corporate policies.

Make sure employees understand that free speech rights don't extend to bloggers, and that violation of the organization's rules and policies—at work or home—may result in the blogger's termination.

Guard Professional (and Personal) Secrets

Protect your organization's trade secrets and your employees' privacy by enforcing rules governing the posting of confidential information on employees' business and personal blogs. Do not allow employee-bloggers to post any content that could embarrass or otherwise harm the organization and its executives, employees, clients, partners, or suppliers. Do not allow employees to violate copyright law by posting copyright-protected material without written permission from the copyright owner.

Support your blog policy with employee training that's designed to educate employees about trade secrets, confidentiality, copyright, and privacy, among other issues. Make sure employees understand what information the organization classifies as confidential data, trade secrets, intellectual property, and so on, and what penalties—up to and including termination—await policy violators.

Prohibit Anonymous Blogging

Do not allow employees to post anonymously by using pseudonyms or fake screen names. Anonymity creates an atmosphere in which some people might be tempted to write in an irresponsible, offensive, harassing, defamatory, or otherwise inappropriate manner. It also runs counter to the blogosphere's honest and transparent nature.

If employees are writing about business on a business blog, they should identify themselves as employees of the company. When employees write about business on personal blogs (strictly in compliance with the organization's rules and policies), their identities and affiliations with the company should be disclosed—along with a legal disclaimer stating that the blogger's comments and opinions belong to the blogger, and are not necessarily shared by the organization.

The courts have not responded consistently to organizations that have attempted to force Internet service providers to disclose the identities of anonymous bloggers who have posted allegedly defamatory statements.[6] Until the courts weigh in formally on this issue, it is in the organization's best interest to use policy to outlaw the use of pseudonyms on business blogs, as well as personal blogs that can adversely affect the organization in any way.

Instruct Bloggers to Use a Legal Disclaimer

Require employees who operate personal blogs or post personal comments on the organization's business blog to incorporate a legal disclaimer stating that their views and opinions are their own and are not necessarily representative of the organization's views and opinions. IBM, for example, requires employee-bloggers to post this disclaimer: "The postings on this site are my own and don't necessarily represent IBM's positions, strategies, or opinions."[7] It is unclear how much protection a legal disclaimer would give the organization in the event of a workplace lawsuit, [8] but it certainly cannot hurt your situation.

Inform Bloggers on How to Handle Media Inquiries

Your organization's business blog program may lead to increased inquiries from the media. In fact, according to the Annual Euro RSCG Magnet and Columbia University Survey, 28 percent of journalists rely on blogs for their daily reporting. Another 70 percent of reporters who use blogs do so to find story ideas, conduct research, and uncover breaking news.[9]

Knowing that employee-bloggers are likely to be contacted directly by reporters, be sure to use your blog policy to instruct bloggers how to handle media calls. Some organizations, for example, want employee-bloggers to route all media inquiries to the organization's public relations department. To be safe, consider putting all bloggers through formal media training so they are prepared to properly handle any media inquiries that may come in as a result of their posts.

Impose Financial Rules

Publicly traded companies must be careful that employee-bloggers do not accidentally or intentionally disclose confidential financial material at the wrong time to the wrong audiences. Make sure employees with access to financial data and investor relations information are thoroughly informed, through written policy and formal training, about what may and may not be revealed to external audiences—and what penalties await organizations and employees who violate regulatory and organizational content and disclosure rules.

Require Bloggers to Keep Retention Policy in Mind

Blog posts and comments can create written business records that the organization must retain and archive for business, legal, and regulatory purposes. Use your organization's blog rules and retention policy to remind employees that, when writing blog posts and comments, they should be mindful of the fact that their written content may need to be retained and turned over to the courts or regulators one day. Stress the fact that business blogs call for professional, business-oriented content, content that will not harm the organization (or the individual blogger) in the event that it one day becomes part of a litigator's evidence pool.

Instruct Employees on How to Handle Comment Spam and Splog

Use written policy to instruct employee-bloggers that, when using the organization's business blogs, they are never to click on comment spam or splog links. Also notify employees that they are prohibited from spamming or splogging via the organization's business blogs or their own personal blogs. Let staff know that employees who engage in comment spamming or splogging will be terminated and may also face criminal or civil prosecution.

Be Sure to Notify Employees of Your Corporate Blog Policy

There is no point having a policy if no one knows about it. According to one recent survey, 94 percent of workers in the United Kingdom report that they have not been informed of their employers' policies on blogs. Another 64 percent believe that employers should not be allowed to fire employees for blogging about their companies.[10] Perhaps if employers did a more effective job of explaining blog-related risks, rules, policies, and procedures to their employees, then employee-bloggers would have a clearer understanding of their rights, along with employers' responsibilities.

The introduction of your organization's blog policy program is a good time to remind employees of all of the organization's employment policies, including harassment and discrimination guidelines, confidentiality agreements, ethics rules, and employee codes of conduct. Make sure employees understand that, regardless of whether employees are blogging, e-mailing, or talking on the phone—the rules are the rules and a violation is a violation.

Use Technology to Help Manage Your People Problems

If you are monitoring employees' business and personal blogs, use your policy to inform them of that. Be sure to secure signed and dated consent forms from employees, acknowledging that they have given management permission to monitor their business and personal blog activity.[11] Sometimes just the knowledge that "Big Brother" is reading over their electronic shoulders is enough to keep employees in line when they are online.

Require Employees to Formally Acknowledge Blog Rules and Policy

Require all employees to sign and date an acknowledgment form, attesting to the fact that they have read the organization's blog policy (including retention and monitoring rules and procedures), understand it, and agree to comply with it or accept the consequences, up to and including termination. Ideally, the acknowledgment process should take place at the conclusion of formal employee training. Keep hard copies of all employee acknowledgment forms on file with the compliance officer or human resources manager. In the event of a workplace lawsuit, you may need signed and dated employee acknowledgment forms to demonstrate the fact that the organization takes blog policy and employee compliance seriously.

Recap and Blog Action Plan

1. Whether your organization opts to operate blogs internally (for employees' eyes only) or externally (for customers and the world to read), it is essential that you establish written blog rules and policies to support and enforce your strategic blog management program.

2. Limit liability somewhat by developing and implementing comprehensive blog rules and policies that address issues including content, language, confidentiality, copyright, defamation, privacy, monitoring, compliance, personal use, retention, regulatory rules, and disciplinary action, among others.

3. Put best practices to work by focusing on the *three Es of blog risk management:* (1) establish policy; (2) educate employees; and (3) enforce policy with discipline, coupled with blog content management and monitoring technology.

4. Distribute a hard copy of the organization's written blog policy to all employee-bloggers, including the CEO and other senior executives who may be blogging. Insist that all employees sign and date a hard copy of the policy, acknowledging that they have read the policy, understand it, and agree to comply with all the organization's blog-related rules and policies or accept disciplinary action, up to and including termination.

5. If you have any doubt about your employees' willingness to adhere to the organization's blog usage and content rules, consider applying a technological solution (content management and monitoring tools) to what essentially is a people problem.

CHAPTER 10

COMMUNICATION IS KEY TO COMPLIANCE

Train, Train, and Train Some More

In the tabloid age, people think that they can say what they want. This is not (covered) by free speech . . . you can't just say what you want.

—*Asbury Park Press*[1]

The Courts Appreciate Proactive, Education-Minded Employers

Although there is no such thing as an entirely risk-free business blog (accidents happen and rogue employees may intentionally trigger disasters), employers who want to ensure that employees' blog posts are as clean and compliant as possible are urged to back up their written blog policy with employee education.

Most employers drop the ball when it comes to educating employees about electronic risks and rules. Just slightly more than half of all employers (54 percent) surveyed in 2004 said they conduct formal e-mail policy training for employees.[2] On the plus side, however, e-policy training has more than doubled since 2001, when only 24 percent of employers offered e-policy education to employees.[3]

As detailed in Chapter 6, based on the legal principle known as *vicarious liability,* an employer may be held responsible for the accidental or intentional misconduct of its employees.[4] That said, the courts and regulators appreciate—and tend to respond favorably to—comprehensive written policy and formal employee education consistently applied.

Your organization may one day need to prove to the court that it is indeed fully committed to a formal, comprehensive blog risk-management program that includes written policy, employee training, and enforcement. To that end, be sure to require all employee-bloggers to sign and date an acknowledgment form confirming that they have undergone blog policy training; they understand the organization's blog rules, policies, and procedures; and they agree to comply with the organization's blog rules and policies—or accept the consequences, up to and including their termination.

Be sure to maintain complete records of the organization's blog training materials. Save, store, and (in the event of a lawsuit) be prepared to quickly produce the following materials:

- Written blog rules and policies (Date and number every new edition.)
- Blog-related training literature and materials: instructor/trainer manuals and scripts; participant workbooks; PowerPoint presentations and scripts; handout materials, etc.
- Employee acknowledgment forms, signed and dated by every employee who has attended blog policy training
- Videotapes and/or audiotapes of training sessions
- Archived webcasts of online training
- Any other records related to the organization's business blog training program

Use Your Organization's Blog Rules and Policies as the Foundation for Training

To be an effective part of your blog management program, continuing employee education must work in concert with your organization's written rules and policies. The most effective training is comprehensive and ongoing. Depending on your organization's blog-related risks, rules, regulations, resources, policies, and procedures, employee training might address the following:

- *Blog Risks and Liabilities.* Review the blog-related risks (workplace lawsuits, regulatory investigations and fines, security breaches, trade secret violations, lost productivity, blog mob attacks, negative publicity, employee termination, etc.) that face the organization, the industry, and individual employee-bloggers.

• *Blog Content.* Explain that business blogs exist primarily for business purposes. Review the type of content, including language and topics, that employee-bloggers are permitted to use (and are prohibited from using) when blogging at the office or at home.

• *Sexual Harassment and Discrimination Guidelines.* Inappropriate blog posts can trigger claims of sexual harassment, sexual discrimination, and hostile work environment, among other legal claims. Make sure employees are aware of the organization's sexual harassment and discrimination guidelines and understand how those guidelines apply to blog posts that are published by employees at the office and at home.

• *Ethics Rules and Employee Code of Conduct.* Familiarize employees with the organization's ethics rules and employee code of conduct. Make sure employees understand that those guidelines also apply to employee blog use at the office and at home.

• *Copyright Law.* Define *copyright* for employees who may not understand the principle of copyright protection. Review copyright law, copyright infringement, and the penalties facing the organization and individual bloggers for posting copyright-protected material without permission of the copyright holder.

• *Trade Secrets and Confidential Information.* Don't assume that all employees know what type of material the organization regards as confidential or otherwise valuable. Define the terms *trade secret, confidential, proprietary,* and *intellectual property.* Explain how confidential material belonging to the organization, business partners, customers, and other third parties is to be handled in the blogosphere. Discuss the organization's legal and financial risks should trade secrets be revealed. Explain the risks that individual bloggers face (disciplinary action, termination, lawsuits) for revealing trade secrets on the organization's business blog or the violator's own personal blog.

• *First Amendment and Privacy Issues.* When it comes to freedom of speech, privacy, and ownership, many bloggers are misguided—dangerously so. Review employees' rights when blogging at the office or at home, as well as the organization's rules and responsibilities. Let employees know, among other things, that bloggers do not have a constitutional right to write anything they want about anyone they want anytime they want. Define *defamation* and explain the risks inherent in a defamatory blog post—including employee termination.

If your organization operates in an employment-at-will state, explain what that means in terms of employees' job security. Be certain that employees understand that management can—and will—fire employees who post blog content (at the office using the organization's computer system or at home on the employee's own time and equipment) that violates any of the organization's written rules and policies.

• *Monitoring Concerns.* Notify employees that the organization has the legal right to monitor business and personal blogs. Inform employees that they have no reasonable expectation of privacy when blogging during working hours or at home on their own time. Communicate the fact that employees who violate the organization's blog rules and policies (or any of the company's written employee guidelines) are subject to disciplinary action, up to and including termination.

• *Blog Business Records.* Explain exactly what a business record is, why it is essential for the organization to retain blog business records, what the individual employee's role is in the blog retention process, and how, in the event of a lawsuit, an employee's inappropriate or objectionable blog content could potentially return one day to harm the organization and embarrass the individual.

• *Regulatory Rules.* Make sure regulated employees are familiar and compliant with regulators' blog-related usage, content, and retention rules.

• *Business Blog Benefits.* Discuss how the organization and individual employee-bloggers can make the most effective and successful use of business blogs.

• *Blog Writers Training.* Successful blog writing is different from other types of business writing. Inform employee-bloggers of the need to post new material on a frequent basis—ideally daily, but certainly no less often than once a week. Review the elements of blog writing style. Instruct business bloggers to write in a conversational, first-person style. Don't forget to cover mechanics. Everything your employees write, whether electronic or traditional, reflects on the organization's credibility and the writer's professionalism. That means spelling, grammar, and punctuation are still as important as ever, even in copy that's published in the ultra-casual blogosphere.

• *Comment Spam and Splog.* Educate employees about blog spam. Explain how and why comment spammers and sploggers operate. Teach employees how to recognize comment spam and splogs. Instruct employees that they are never to click on an outgoing link from splog or comment spam. Make it clear that employees are prohibited from splogging and comment spamming from the organization's blogs or their own personal blogs. Stress the fact that employees who engage in blog spamming face disciplinary action, up to and including termination.

Recap and Blog Action Plan

1. The courts and regulators have demonstrated their appreciation for consistent rules and policies that are supported by comprehensive employee training.
2. A combination of written blog rules and policies, plus employee education and technology tools, may motivate compliance and help prevent workplace lawsuits and other blog risks.
3. Formal blog rules and written blog policies are the foundation of employee education.
4. Approach blog policy training as an ongoing, continuing education program—not a one-time-only event.
5. Educate every employee-blogger. If the CEO and other senior executives are blogging, they need to undergo training, too.
6. As part of the organization's blog-policy training program, stress the fact that blog rules and policies (along with all of the organization's other employment policies) apply, regardless of whether employees are blogging at the office on company time or at home on their own time with their own equipment.
7. Conclude training by requiring all employees to sign and date an acknowledgment form confirming that they have undergone blog policy training; understand the organization's blog rules, policies, and procedures; and agree to comply with the organization's blog rules and policies—or accept disciplinary action, up to and including termination.
8. You may one day need to prove to the court that your organization is fully committed to a formal, comprehensive blog risk-management program that includes written policy, employee training, and enforcement. Save, store, and (if subpoenaed) produce all literature, materials, and records related to the organization's business blog training program.

PART 4

THE BLOG IS ALL ABOUT CONTENT

CHAPTER 11

CONTENT CAN MAKE—OR BREAK—YOUR BLOG AND YOUR BUSINESS

If you're only in business to make money, you probably don't need a blog. If you have a corporate mission, a blog keeps you engaged with the world.

—Christine Halvorson, chief blogger, Stonyfield Farm[1]

The blog is all about content. So much so that, "a small but growing" number of organizations are now hiring professionals to write blogs "in a conversational style about timely topics that would appeal to customers, clients, and potential recruits," according to the *Wall Street Journal*.[2] Annual salaries for corporate bloggers range from $40,000 to $70,000. Responsibilities typically include creating, writing, and promoting the corporate blog, as well as creating links to related blogs.[3]

In addition, many companies have expanded the duties of existing marketing, public relations, or IT professionals (who happen to be interested in and savvy about blogs) to include business blogging. The goal: Ensure that the organization's business blog contains compelling yet conversational content, expresses the "feel" of the organization, helps build relationships with key audiences, and captures the attention of blog search engines.

As the following real-life blog disaster story illustrates, companies are wise to invest the financial and human resources necessary to ensure that their business blogs send "the right" message about the company to "the right" audience. One misstep is all it takes to trigger a blogstorm that can significantly damage (and perhaps destroy) your business.

BLOG RULE #20: The blog is all about content.

The Blogosphere Hates a Phony!

What separates a successful business blog from an effective corporate web page is, in part, the heartfelt honesty, the transparency, of the content. If your organization has a social cause to promote, a corporate philosophy to communicate, or a compelling story to tell, then a business blog may be the ideal communications channel for you.

On the other hand, blogs that are written by dispassionate marketing professionals who are simply going through the motions of writing copy to generate sales are destined for failure, public ridicule—and perhaps attack—in the blogosphere.

BLOG RULE #21: Blogging culture demands absolute honesty. The blogosphere hates a phony!

Mazda: Crashing and Burning in the Blogosphere

Take the case of Mazda's ill-fated attempt to use the blogosphere to reach Gen Y buyers, the generation of 57 million young people born between 1981 and 1995, who are said to create the largest consumer group in the history of the United States.[4]

As reported by *Fortune*,[5] Mazda, as part of its Gen Y marketing efforts, created a blog that was supposedly run by a hip 22-year-old named Kid Halloween. On the blog, Kid Halloween discussed topics and used language designed to appeal to buyers in their teens and early twenties. He also posted a link to three videos, which he claimed a friend had recorded from public access television, but actually were expensively produced. In one video, a Mazda3 attempted to break dance. Another video showed the car driving off a ramp like a skateboard. Both videos ended with dramatic crashes.

Puzzled by the expensively produced videos and sensing a fraud, bloggers started talking—negatively—about Mazda's blog. Blogging culture, which demands absolute honesty, is quick to pounce on a lie. After three days of getting bashed in the blogosphere, Mazda deactivated its ill-conceived blog.[6]

Stonyfield Farm: Spreading the Gospel of Healthy Eating Throughout the Blogosphere

At the opposite end of the transparency spectrum is Stonyfield Farm's blog program.[7] The organic yogurt manufacturer proves that you don't have to be a publicly traded multinational giant like IBM or a technology titan like Sun Microsystems to operate a successful blog program. Any company, public or private, large or small, can succeed in the blogosphere—if you have something genuine to say, and you know how to say it.

New Hampshire-based Stonyfield Farm, the world's largest organic yogurt manufacturer, is a privately held company that grew from a few hippies committed to healthy eating to some 314 employees and a customer base of confirmed yogurt lovers.

Structuring its blog program around the company's commitment to "healthy food, healthy people, and a healthy planet,"[8] Stonyfield Farm has received widespread recognition, including a *BusinessWeek Online* cover story,[9] for its successful blog culture, the brainchild of CEO Gary Hirshberg.

Under the direction of former journalist and chief blogger Christine Halvorson, Stonyfield Farm operates two blogs (Baby Babble and The Bovine Bugle), which are directed toward customers and other external audiences, as well as employees. Halvorson, who also holds the title of web editor/writer, writes most of the Baby Babble posts herself. The Bovine Bugle is written by the proprietor of Howmars Farm, a certified organic dairy farm located in Franklin, Vermont.[10]

Readers' Comments Solicited—Safely

As part of its blog program, Stonyfield Farm solicits comments from employees, customers, and other third parties. The first line of blog defense for Stonyfield Farm, Halvorson is responsible for previewing the comments of employees and third parties to ensure that neither factually incorrect material nor personally abusive comments are posted. In addition, the chief blogger edits contributors' comments for style, ensuring that grammar and punctuation are correct and that posts are logical and readable.

Employers who want to minimize blog risks are advised to follow Stonyfield Farm's lead and assign either a public relations professional, chief blogger, or other responsible party to review, edit, and—as necessary—delete all comments pre-post. Remember, everyone who writes a blog or contributes to a blog's comment section has a voice—a potentially dangerous voice. All it takes is one inappropriate comment to trigger a workplace lawsuit, regulatory investigation, or blog mob attack. In spite of the blo-gosphere's call for unedited, unmanaged, "pure" content, savvy employers are advised to protect their organizations by either deactivating or modify-ing the comment function of the organization's blog software, requiring readers to register before commenting, or manually editing comments pre-post for the sake of the organization's reputation and future.

> **BLOG RULE #22:** Assign a lawyer or other responsible party to review, edit, and—as necessary—delete readers' comments pre-post. All it takes is one inappropriate comment to trigger a workplace lawsuit, reg-ulatory investigation, or blog mob attack.

An Interactive Communications Tool for a Socially Active Company

Stonyfield Farm launched its blog program as an opportunity to talk in a very personal way with customers, and thereby maintain a personal con-nection with consumers. Never an organization to follow the traditional marketing path, Stonyfield Farm was an early adopter of the business blog. Not surprising. The company, which sells 18 million cups of yogurt a month,[11] was among the first food manufacturers to print socially active statements like "Go Save the Environment" on its yogurt lids.

The blog is yet another nontraditional marketing tool that allows a smaller company like Stonyfield Farm to create an "immediate intimate connection" with consumers. As CEO Hirshberg told *BusinessWeek On-line,* blogging enables Stonyfield Farm to build consumer loyalty without spending millions of dollars on mainstream media advertising.[12]

> **BLOG RULE #23:** Blogs allow smaller companies to create immediate intimate connections with consumers and build loyalty without spend-ing millions of dollars on traditional mainstream media advertising.

Connecting Emotionally with Customers: Giving Readers a Voice

Hirshberg attributes the company's growth to its "emotional connection with customers." According to the CEO, Stonyfield Farm is "growing at four times category rate in some markets and three times the category rate nationally."[13]

Through its blogs, Stonyfield Farm is able to tap into, and act upon, consumer opinions—right now. For example, when the company was searching for a pediatrician to partner with, readers of the Baby Babble blog were polled to determine who the most trusted authority is among parents of babies and toddlers. The immediate feedback led Stonyfield Farm to a candidate for its pediatrician-spokesperson position. A traditional survey or on-site focus group, by contrast, would have taken weeks to organize, conduct, analyze, and act upon.[14]

Seven Blogging Content and Management Tips from Stonyfield Farm[15]

1. Be real. Be funny. Exude a personality. Express opinions. Be authentic. Don't bore people. Readers will see through you if you act otherwise.
2. If you think you have to blog because everyone else is blogging, don't do it. If you really have something to say, a blog is an excellent tool. It's not just one more place to toot your horn or issue a press release. Blog readers won't tolerate that for long.
3. Constant updating is a must.
4. Control spam before it starts. This should be your chief deciding factor when determining which blogging software or application to use.
5. Give readers something to do once they visit, other than read your (ideally) compelling prose. For example, give readers the opportunity to print out a coupon, subscribe to an e-newsletter, contribute a comment, voice an opinion, or download a timely article.
6. Remember: If you ask for comments, people will comment. Be prepared. Blogging culture is not necessarily polite, but it is honest.
7. Consider a trial run. Experiment with trial postings before you announce to the world that your organization's blog is up and running.

Recap and Blog Action Plan

1. The blog is all about content. Make sure your organization's business blog contains compelling yet conversational content, expresses

the "feel" of the organization, helps build relationships with key
audiences, and captures the attention of blog search engines.

2. What separates a successful business blog from an effective corporate web page is, in part, the heartfelt honesty and the transparency
   of the content.

3. Blogs that are written for the purpose of sales and marketing are
   destined for failure, public ridicule, and—perhaps—attack in the
   blogosphere. The blogosphere hates a phony.

4. Blogs give readers a voice, enabling the organization to tap into
   and act upon consumer opinions—right now.

5. To minimize blog risks, assign either a lawyer, public relations professional, chief blogger, or other responsible party to review, edit,
   and—as necessary—delete reader comments pre-post.

CHAPTER 12

MANAGING AND EDITING WRITERS' POSTS AND READERS' COMMENTS

If you fudge or lie on a blog, you are biting the karmic weenie.
—Steve Hayden, Ogilvy & Mather vice chairman, quoted in *Fortune*[1]

One roadblock to business blogging may be employers' understandable concerns about unmanaged and potentially dangerous content. Among organizations that have yet to adopt blogging, 22 percent say they fear losing control of their company's message in the blogosphere, and another 22 percent express concern over what employee-bloggers might write.[2]

Although employers' fears over potentially dangerous and damaging content are certainly justified, organizations are being shortsighted if they limit their content-related concerns solely to employees. As recent high-profile, headline-generating e-mail gaffes demonstrate, CEOs, lawyers, accountants, and other executives and professionals are as capable as any other employee of writing ill-conceived and ultimately disastrous electronic content.

Inappropriate content is inappropriate content, whether it's written by a C-level executive or an entry-level employee, transmitted via e-mail, or posted (and permalinked) on a blog. The primary difference is that risky blog content has a never-ending "viral" quality. You can count on a juicy, salacious, or otherwise unprofessional or embarrassing blog post to be read, linked to, and commented upon by countless readers for years to come. In fact, thanks to the permalink, blog posts have the potential to reside in the blogosphere forever. There simply is no taking your words back once your post goes live.

BLOG RULE #24: Inappropriate content is inappropriate content, whether it's transmitted via e-mail or posted (and permalinked) on a blog. The primary difference is that risky blog content has a never-ending "viral" quality. You can count on a juicy, salacious, or otherwise unprofessional and embarrassing blog post to be read, linked to, and commented upon by countless readers for years to come.

Don't Allow Employees to Play Fast and Loose with Content

As a rule, the more casual the technology, the less professional the writer's content tends to be. For example, research shows that employees tend to play fast and loose with content when they use business IM—a decidedly more casual form of communication than e-mail.

According to the 2004 Workplace E-Mail and Instant Messaging Survey from American Management Association and The ePolicy Institute, some employees put the organization at tremendous risk of legal claims and security breaches when they engage in workplace IM:

- Fifty-eight percent of workers engage in personal IM chat at the office.
- Sixteen percent of employees admit to transmitting jokes, gossip, rumors, and disparaging remarks via IM.
- Nine percent of workplace IM users have used the technology to transmit confidential company information.
- Six percent of employees confess to engaging in sexual, romantic, or pornographic IM chat during the work day.[3]

Employees already are using IM to violate content policy, transmit company secrets, and chat about the type of topics that tend to trigger lawsuits and provide litigators with valuable "smoking gun" evidence of wrongdoing. Why assume they will take a more professional and compliant approach to business blogging?

Protect Hard-Won Relationships with Content and Language Rules

Why is it so important to provide employee-bloggers with guidelines to control language and content on personal and business blogs? To protect the organization's hard-won relationships with customers, for one thing. As any sales professional will attest, it is a lot harder and much more costly to win a new client than it is to hold on to existing customers—unless, of course, your employees are busy alienating current clients in the blogosphere.

Business Cannot Afford to Be Bullied by the Blogosphere

Blogging, by its nature, is even more casual, conversational, and potentially calamitous than instant messaging or e-mail. The blogosphere encourages honest, unfiltered, "pure" commentary. The blogosphere tends to recoil at the suggestion of pre-post editing by lawyers or managers.

Do not allow the blogosphere to bully you into court and out of business. Use a combination of written content and netiquette rules, plus training and technology tools to keep bloggers' content clean and compliant.

That is not to suggest that the organization should wring the life out of employee and CEO blogs. The most successful, well-read bloggers are those who are not afraid to inject some personality into their writing and to take a stand on the issues they care about. That is fine. Just be sure, however, that your organization's business bloggers balance their passion with professionalism. That means no name calling, no mudslinging, no attacks on those who do not share your point of view. In other words, no violation of any of the organization's rules and policies, period.

Edit Posts and Comments with Care

Given the risks inherent in business blogging, employers are advised to screen writers' posts and readers' comments pre-post to avoid publishing content that is defamatory or inaccurate, violates copyright law, reveals confidential information, or otherwise is inappropriate, offensive, or in violation of rules, regulations, and policies.

You can prescreen content manually or automatically with content management and aggregation software. You also can modify your comment feature to require registration before readers are allowed to post comments.

Reject any posts or comments that fail to pass the "smell test." For all others, be sure to edit with care. Feel free to correct mechanical errors (spelling, grammar, and punctuation), and suggest copy changes to your employees to enhance a post's readability.

Treat Readers and Commenters with Respect

As Stonyfield Farm's chief blogger noted in Chapter 11, "Remember, if you ask for comments, people will comment. Be prepared. Blogging culture is not necessarily polite, but it is honest,"[4] If a reader takes time to post a comment or send an e-mail in response to a blog post, be responsive and gracious. You are not required to publish every comment that comes your way (particularly if a third party's comment is untruthful, unkind, or otherwise likely to create legal problems or concerns for the organization). However, you are obligated to treat every reader and correspondent with professional courtesy.

Review Sexual Harassment and Discrimination Policies with Bloggers

Because of the relaxed, informal nature of blogs, some employees will put in writing comments they never would say aloud. Make sure employees understand that, regardless of how they are published or transmitted, comments that are of a sexual nature, or comments that disparage anyone because of race, religion, age, color, national origin, disability, or political belief are strictly forbidden. All it takes is one offensive post to land your organization on the wrong side of an expensive, protracted sexual harassment or discrimination claim.

Educate All Employees—From the Intern to the CEO

New hires and long-time employees, the CEO, senior executives, managers and supervisors, full-time professionals and part-time staff, telecommuters and temporary employees, independent contractors and freelancers—everyone should be informed of the company's blog usage, content, and netiquette policies.

Make your blog policy and disciplinary rules one-size-fits-all. Policy is policy, compliance is compliance, violations are violations, and discipline is discipline—regardless of the blogger's title or rank.

Recap and Blog Action Plan

1. Among nonblogging organizations, 22 percent fear losing control of their company's message, and another 22 percent express concern over what employee-bloggers might write.[5]

2. A CEO's inappropriate post is more likely to shine a negative light on the organization than is a post written by any other employee.
3. Inappropriate content is inappropriate content, whether it's transmitted via e-mail or posted (and permalinked) on a blog.
4. Do not allow the blogosphere to bully you into court and out of business.
5. Use policy, training, and technology to manage blog content.
6. Edit writers' posts and readers' comments with care.
7. Educate all employees, from interns to C-level executives, about usage, content, and netiquette policies.

CHAPTER 13

BLOG ETIQUETTE, OR NETIQUETTE

Twelve Tips to Help Maximize Civil Discourse

Imagine dropping your diary on the street somewhere, and the next day, it's world news.

—JESSICA CUTLER, FORMER SENATE AIDE WHOSE WASHINGTONIENNE BLOG SCANDALIZED CAPITOL HILL[1]

Every blog entry that is posted by an employee reflects on the organization's credibility and the professionalism of the writer. Blog posts that are illogical, poorly constructed, or riddled with mechanical errors can turn off readers and stall careers. Blog posts that intentionally or accidentally betray confidences, reveal trade secrets, or disclose financial information can trigger lawsuits and regulatory investigations. Blog posts that are menacing, harassing, pornographic, defamatory, discriminatory, or otherwise inappropriate can lead to terminations, litigation, and negative publicity.

An effective blog policy should incorporate a discussion of the rules of *netiquette,* or electronic etiquette. By addressing and enforcing the rules of blog etiquette, employers can maximize civil business behavior in the blogosphere while minimizing the likelihood that employee-bloggers will write inappropriate or offensive entries that might turn off readers, trigger litigation, or otherwise harm the organization.

BLOG RULE #25: Incorporate the rules of blog etiquette into the organization's blog policy. By addressing and enforcing blog etiquette, employers can maximize civil business behavior in the blogosphere while minimizing the likelihood of inappropriate entries that might offend readers, trigger litigation, or otherwise harm the organization.

This chapter offers a dozen important tips that you should consider incorporating into your organization's blog etiquette guidelines.

Tip 1. Think Before You Speak in Public

Once the words are out of your mouth, they're out of your control. Never has that been truer than in the age of blogs. Today, an ill-considered comment that is uttered in a public forum can spark an immediate, heated, and career-altering response from the blogosphere.

Take the case of Neil French, "one of the world's most flamboyant advertising gurus."[2] French learned this lesson the hard way when, during a presentation at an advertising industry conference, he sparking an ad industry blogstorm by calling women "crap" and noting that a woman "can't be a great creative director and have a baby and keep spending time off every time your kids are ill."[3]

The fallout from French's speech, and the ensuing blogstorm, included his resignation as creative director of the worldwide advertising giant WPP Group. Blaming bloggers for the industry uproar over his sexist comments, French noted, "Death by blog is not really the way to go."[4]

Tip 2. Be Discreet—Be Professional—Be Mindful of the Future

Although it's true that a blog is defined as an online diary, please don't consider that an invitation to share your most private thoughts or fantasies, reveal secret fetishes and personal peccadilloes, or post indiscreet photos of yourself in questionable poses or outlandish attire. Everything you write for public consumption, whether posted on a blog or printed on paper, reflects on your individual professionalism and your organization's credibility.

Just as many of us tend to judge strangers on the basis of appearance, so too do readers understandably assess the person behind the blog on the basis of the posts published. That's why some employers now check out job applicants' blogs.[5] They are hoping to catch a glimpse of the "real" person hiding behind the polished and professional resume.

Tip 3. Need Therapy? Don't Write a Blog: Seek Counseling Instead

Nearly 50 percent of bloggers consider blogging to be form of self-therapy. Another 31 percent of bloggers turn to writing in their blogs or reading others' blogs in times of high anxiety, rather than seeking professional counseling, according to a Digital Marketing Services survey.[6]

Bad idea! The public blogosphere is no place to communicate the type of private thoughts that should more appropriately be reserved for therapy. Remember, blog posts can create written business records that must be retained for legal, regulatory, and management reasons. What you write today could one day come back to haunt you, embarrass your loved ones, and damage your employer in the event of a workplace lawsuit or regulatory investigation. If your blog posts or comments are subpoenaed as part of the discovery process, they will be entered into the record—for lawyers, jurors, reporters, your employer, the media, and others to see. Professional counseling, by contrast, is a private matter that will always remain private.

Tip 4. Don't Use Your Blog to Let Off Steam

Compose yourself before composing your blog entries. If you wouldn't say it to a person's face, don't post it on a blog. Unlike watercooler gossip sessions and face-to-face confrontations, a verbal battle that is played out in the blogosphere creates written history. Thanks to permalinks, an ugly blog post can remain in the blogosphere forever, generating hard feelings, negative publicity, and other unpleasant consequences for all concerned—for a long time to come.

Take the case of New Zealand National Member of Parliament Murray McCully. As reported by the *New Zealand Herald*, McCully came under fire for referring to Department of Labor Secretary Dr. James Buwalda as "Dr. Bewildered" in his blog. McCully's name calling is considered particularly abusive because civil servants in New Zealand are not permitted to respond to criticism (even name calling) by politicians. Nonetheless, the *New Zealand Herald* reports that McCully "will not be swayed," in spite of warnings from the state services commissioner to stop the name calling.[7]

Business blogs exist primarily for business purposes. There is no place for language that is hostile, blunt, rude, obscene, insensitive, abusive, menacing, harassing, discriminatory, or otherwise nasty or offensive on a business blog—or a personal blog, for that matter.

Tip 5. Watch Your Language

Ill-advised blog comments could lead to a legal claims, monetary fines, and jail time. Consider the case of Patrick DePula, a former Wisconsin county supervisor who pled guilty to a charge of e-mail defamation after using the county e-mail system to send a message alleging that another county supervisor was an aficionado of bestiality. Facing a possible sentence of nine months in jail plus a $10,000 fine, DePula ultimately was fined $1,000 by the court and ordered to perform 250 hours of community service.[8]

The case, which "sent ripples through city and county governments,"[9] should serve as a warning to bloggers who may be tempted to use the power of the blog to snipe at, gossip about, or otherwise defame coworkers—or anyone else, for that matter. Before you publish rumors, gossip, or a defamatory remark, stop to consider whether that post is really worth a five-figure fine and months behind bars.

Tip 6. Don't Blog Anonymously: Stand Behind Your Posted Opinions

Let's face it, anonymity creates an atmosphere in which some people might be tempted to write in an irresponsible, offensive, harassing, defamatory, or otherwise inappropriate manner. At the end of the day, there is no guarantee that anonymous blogging will protect hidden writers from detection, anyway.

St. Louis Post-Dispatch reporter Daniel Finney learned this lesson the hard way when he was suspended from his job after posting "lengthy passages about his job as a Post-Dispatch features writer" on his personal blog—under the pseudonym Roland H. Thompson.

In his anonymous personal blog, "Roland H. Thompson" took "frequent, thinly veiled potshots against his employer and coworkers." He also wrote about his assignments for the paper. One example, reported by Riverfront Times: "Today was an absolute abomination. It began unwittingly at 7:30 A.M. when I was forced from my sweet, gentle slumber to go work on a hideously lame story involving Santa Claus and the Hard Rock Café."[10]

In another case of anonymous blogging, a male blogger who had successfully operated a popular blog for 18 months under a female pseudonym actually outed himself. For a year and a half, Assistant U.S. Attorney David Lat used his dishy blog, Underneath Their Robes, to gossip about federal judges under the guise of a female lawyer named Article III Groupie. Lat finally ended his anonymity in a story in the New Yorker. He told the magazine that he was revealing his true identity because the successful blog left him feeling "frustrated that I was putting a lot of time into this and was unable to get any credit for it."[11]

According to the *New Jersey Law Journal*, Lat did receive "credit" from his employer once his identity was revealed. In accordance with his superior, Lat deactivated Underneath Their Robes shortly after the *New Yorker* hit newsstands. The blog, which violated policy requiring assistant U.S. attorneys to get approval before talking with the media, may have ongoing fallout. As Lat told the *New Yorker*, "I only hope the judges I appear in front of don't read it."[12]

Finally, consider the case of Heather Armstrong, the blogger who is credited with coining the term *dooced,* which means to lose your job for blogging. According to the *New York Times,* Armstrong used her blog, Dooce.com, to complain "colorfully about everything from her boss to obnoxious coworkers." In 2002, she lost her position as a web designer after referring to her boss as "Her Wretchedness," and "the most insane person you have ever witnessed outside of 'Dateline NBC,'" among other comments.[13] Although Armstrong never revealed the name of her employer, one reader did not share her sense of discretion. That reader not only figured out where Armstrong worked, but also followed up with an e-mail to Armstrong's employer, detailing the nature of the blogger's rants. Armstrong was fired immediately.[14]

A legal note: The courts have not responded consistently to organizations that have attempted to force Internet service providers to disclose the identities of anonymous bloggers who have posted allegedly defamatory statements.[15] Until the courts formally weigh in on this issue, it is in the best interest of both the individual blogger and the organization to steer clear of pseudonyms, whether the blog is for business or personal use.

Tip 7. Do Your Homework Before Joining a Blog Mob

Orchestrated blog attacks can be devastating to businesses and individuals. Blogstorms have tarnished corporate reputations, triggered declines in stock valuations, generated negative publicity, and cost people their jobs.

Regardless of how strong you feel about an issue, think twice before joining a blog mob. Do your homework. Make sure you have all the facts straight before publishing negative, critical, or hurtful posts or comments about a person, product, or organization. You cannot believe everything you read online, so be sure your sources are reliable before acting on information that could ultimately prove to be idle gossip or a flat-out lie.

Tip 8. Don't Comment Unless You Have Something Legitimate to Add to the Conversation

Just as unnecessary e-mail copies (Cc) and blind carbon copies (Bcc) waste everyone's time, so too do casual remarks that are unnecessarily posted to the comment section of blogs. Conserve your time and energy, and save the blog publisher's space, by commenting only when you have something legitimate, timely, and valuable to add to an online conversation.

Tip 9. Be 100 Percent Honest

Nowhere is honesty more valued than in the blogosphere. Bloggers are unusually adept at uncovering lies—and attacking the liar. Consider "Rathergate," the now-famous episode in which political bloggers questioned the authenticity of memos used by CBS news anchor Dan Rather on the news show *60 Minutes* to "prove" that President George W. Bush was derelict in his duty as a member of the Texas National Guard. The bloggers' efforts to uncover the truth led to CBS disavowing the memos and Rather announcing his retirement.[16] This is an early and unforgettable case of dogged citizen journalists unseating a mainstream media giant.

Tip 10. Keep an Eye on Spelling, Grammar, and Punctuation

Your readers will. You wouldn't walk into the CEO's office, a customer's showroom, or a trade industry conference and start speaking gibberish. Why would you post a blog entry that is illogical, full of mechanical errors, or otherwise a form of written gibberish?

One important goal of business blogging is to attract and grow a loyal following of readers who will turn regularly to your blog as an expert source of timely and truthful information. It's hard to establish that type of influential position if your written communication lacks professionalism and credibility.

Tip 11. Be Gracious to Readers and Commenters

If a reader takes time to post a comment or send an e-mail in response to a blog post, be responsive and gracious. You are not required to publish every comment that comes your way (particularly if a third-party's comment is untruthful, unkind, or otherwise likely to create legal problems or other concerns for the organization). But you are obligated to treat every reader and correspondent with professional courtesy. Confronted by a particularly prickly reader? See the next tip.

Tip 12. Develop a Thick Skin

As the publisher of a business blog, expect to receive a certain amount of negative feedback about your blog and your business. You may even experience some name-calling, as the software firm Marqui did when it launched its "Paybloggers Program" in 2004. Bloggers responded to the program, in which Marqui retained twenty bloggers to write about the company in exchange for a monthly fee of $800, by calling the company names like "pond scum" and "shills."[17]

What's the best way to respond to name-calling in the blogosphere? Unless you have been defamed and have grounds for legal action, the best advice is to simply grow up. Get over it. And continue being gracious to your own readers and commenters.

Recap and Blog Action Plan

1. Use your written blog policy to establish and enforce the rules of blog etiquette, or "netiquette."
2. Use blog etiquette guidelines to help maximize civil business behavior, while minimizing the posting of inappropriate content that could offend readers, trigger litigation, or otherwise harm the organization.

CHAPTER 14

BATTLING COMMENT SPAM AND SPLOG

Uh, ladies and gentlemen of the blogosphere, I think we have an emergency on our hands.

—TIM BRAY, SUN MICROSYSTEMS' WEB TECHNOLOGIES
DIRECTOR AND BLOGGER, TBRAY.ORG [1]

First it was *spam*, or junk e-mail. Then came *spim*, or unsolicited instant messages. Now say hello to *splog*, the blogosphere's term for the unwelcome combination of spam plus blogs.

The blogosphere—whose enthusiasts argue that spam undermines the trust that is at the heart of blogging—in part has itself to blame for the explosion of splog. A phenomenally successful technology, blogging is growing at such breakneck pace that already there are some 34 million blogs operating worldwide.[2] Another 32 million people in the United States alone identify themselves as blog readers.[3] How can spammers resist numbers like that? With blog publishers and readers numbering in the tens of millions (and growing every day), the temptation to splog is proving overwhelming both to spammers and to the blog hosting industry that is struggling to control splog.

Splogging 101

What is a splog? Basically, a splog is a phony blog. Its content is often a combination of copy stolen from legitimate blogs, links to advertisers' websites, and gibberish. Any topic that has ever been spammed about via e-mail (weight loss, hair loss, sexual potency, pornography, to name just a few topics) is now being splogged.

Spam takes two forms in the blogosphere. It may show up on a legitimate blog in the form of comments from fake readers who have nothing to say about the topic at hand. The spammer simply wants to get a sales pitch in front of readers' eyes or con people into clicking on a link to an advertisement-laden website that is unrelated to the blog. This is called *comment spam*. The spammer, who preys on the open, interactive, give-and-take culture of the blogosphere, makes money each time an unsuspecting visitor clicks on a link. Every time someone clicks on an advertiser's link, a comment spammer profits.

The second type of blog spam occurs when a spammer sets up a fake blog, or a *splog*. Once again, the goal is to entice readers to click on links that will take them to advertisements. According to blog search engine Technorati's *State of the Blogosphere* report, 5.8 percent of new blogs, representing about 50,000 posts on average, are phony or potentially phony blogs—splogs, in other words.[4]

How does a splog work? What makes splog so annoying to readers and so dangerous to blog publishers? Let's say, for example, that you are looking for a blog on which an expert gemologist discusses antique jewelry. You turn to a blog search engine for a list of antique jewelry blogs, click on a relevant-sounding site, and are immediately taken to a bogus blog that may contain a few words related to antique jewelry but that really exists to get visitors to link to ads. Both you and the legitimate blogger whose jewelry-related content was pilfered have been splogged.[5]

A "Spamalanche" Buries the Blogosphere

What has been termed a *spamalanche*[6] or *splogsplosion*[7] rocked the blogosphere in October 2005, when the biggest splog attack to date hit Google's Blogger blog-creation tool and its BlogSpot hosting service, the two most popular free blog services available. The assault, which led to "clogged RSS readers and overflowing in-boxes," may have "manipulated search engine rankings" as well.[8] As a result of the spamalanche, Blogger dismantled 13,000 spam-filled blogs in a single weekend.[9]

According to *CNET News.com*, "The scope of the attack, and the sophisticated automation used to accomplish it, mark a turning point for splogging."[10] Compounding the problem is the fact that blogging services, unlike e-mail programs, lack the capacity to easily detect and filter out spam, according to Bob Wyman, chief technology officer at PubSub, a blog search and tracking service.[11]

Google, which was widely attacked in the blogosphere following the October splogsplosion, reports that it is working on the problem. As reported by *Wired News*, Blogger has added a word-verification feature, called Captcha, to the blog-creation process. In addition, Blogger has published a list of detected splog URLs, so they can be removed from the indexes of other search engines.[12]

It is important to note that the blogosphere's spam problem is not restricted to Google's Blogger and BlogSpot. Blogs overall have a problem with comment spam and splog, a problem that is bound to get bigger before it gets better. It is up to both the blog creation and hosting industries, as well as corporate and individual bloggers, to identify and implement anti-spam solutions to help minimize the likelihood of and risks associated with comment spam and splogs.

How to Keep Splogs and Comment Spam from Invading Your Business Blog

Although technology struggles to solve the challenge of surging splog attacks and comment spam, business bloggers (and individuals who are blogging at home) are advised to do what they can on their own to battle spam in the blogosphere. Here are nine tips:

1. *Do not entrust your organization's blog program to free blog creation and hosting services.* Instead, opt for an enterprise blogging solution to operate and manage your business blog. With an enterprise system, you maintain control over content, comments as well as posts, and remain isolated from threats that may be levied at public blog hosting services.

2. *Before committing to blog creation software or a blog hosting service, determine what the vendor's spam-control capabilities are.* What happens to your business if another spamalanche hits and thousands of legitimate blogs are deactivated by the hosting service?

3. *Deactivate or modify the comment feature of your blog program.* If there are no comments coming in, then you can be sure there is no comment spam infiltrating your blog. *Wired News* reports that Movable Type 3.2 and WordPress are two blogging platforms that offer built-in comment moderation options.[13]

4. *Assign someone to review reader comments pre-post and delete comment spam as well as any inappropriate comments that violate the organization's policies*

or would be likely to offend readers. This might be a lawyer, compliance officer, the blog czar, or a public relations professional, for example.

5. *Determine if your organization has been victimized by a splogger.* According to *Wired News*, sploggers may be stealing your legitimate blog content in order to increase their Google rankings—and thereby generate advertising revenue. To find out if your blog copy has been pilfered, subscribe to news feeds at every blog search engine. Search the blogosphere using terms that include your company name, your blog's name, and your URL.[14]

BLOG RULE #26: Use blog monitoring tools to track what is being written about your organization and help control comment spam and splog.

6. *Consider using your written blog policy and IT controls to prohibit employees from visiting blogs outside the organization's firewall.* If employees can't visit outside blogs, they can't link to advertisers' phony splogs and in the process put your organization at risk of viruses, spyware, and other security nightmares.

7. *Report splog attacks.* If you are using a public blog tool like Blogger, let the hosting service know if you come across a splog. If you are using an enterprise blog solution, notify your CIO if you are hit with comment spam or get splogged.

8. *Educate employees about blog spam.* Help clean up the blogosphere by informing employees about splog and comment spam. Let them know what to look for and how to report comment spam or splogs that they encounter at the office or at home.

9. *Use your written blog policy to inform employees that they are prohibited from splogging or comment spamming.* Notify employees that this pertains to both the organization's business blog and their own personal blogs, and that violations of this rule will result in disciplinary action, up to and including termination.

BLOG RULE #27: Although technology struggles to solve the challenge of surging splog attacks and comment spam, business bloggers (and individuals who are blogging at home) are advised to do what they can on their own to battle spam in the blogosphere.

Recap and Blog Action Plan

1. Spam takes two forms in the blogosphere. Comment spam appears on legitimate blogs in the form of phony comments from fake readers with nothing to say. The second type of blog spam occurs when a spammer sets up a fake blog, or splog. In both cases, the spammer's goal is to get readers to click on links to advertisements.

2. Blogging services, unlike e-mail programs, lack the capacity to easily detect and filter out spam.

3. Although technology struggles to address the surge in splog attacks and comment spam, businesses and individuals are advised to do what they can, on their own, to battle spam in the blogosphere.

PART 5

BLOG BACKLASH: EMPLOYERS FIGHT BACK WITH LAWSUITS AND PINK SLIPS

CHAPTER 15

EMPLOYEE-BLOGGERS BEWARE 1: BLOGGING CAN GET YOU FIRED!

A blog can be a great way to vent about work. It can also be an invitation to a pink slip.

— *THE NEW YORK TIMES*[1]

Understand Your Risks, Rights, and Responsibilities Before You Blog

Whether in the courtroom (in the form of lawsuits) or in the pocketbook (in the shape of pink slips), some employers have already demonstrated that they have the wherewithal to fight back when assaulted in the blogosphere.

According to the Society for Human Resource Management, 3 percent of organizations have disciplined employees for blogging.[2] Fully 26 percent of employers have fired employees for misusing the Internet, and another 25 percent have terminated workers for e-mail misuse, according to the 2005 Electronic Monitoring and Surveillance Survey from American Management Association and The ePolicy Institute.[3] As the popularity of blogging grows, expect corresponding growth in policy violations, accompanied by an increase in blog-related discipline, terminations, and litigation.

By far, the biggest risk employee-bloggers face is being fired (or *dooced*, in blog parlance) for their blog content or usage. Recall the example in Chapter 13 of blogger Heather B. Armstrong, who in 2002 was fired for writing about her job and colleagues on her blog, www.dooce.com.[4] To date, there have been hundreds of employees who either have been fired for their blog content or who have tendered their resignations over blog-related issues. Some employees have been fired for inappropriate, offensive, or illegal blog content that they posted while on the job. Others have been dooced for blogging in the privacy of their own homes, on their own time, using their own blog software and computer hardware. Typically, employee-bloggers are dooced because of the negative or unflattering comments they have posted about their employers.

Given the candid, tell-all nature of the blogosphere, it is no surprise that dooced employees have gone online to share their cautionary tales with the blogging community. Sites such as The Bloggers' Rights Blog[5] (rights.journalspace.com), The Papal Bull[6] (homepage.mac.com/popemark/iblog) and Morpheme Tales[7] (committeetoprotectbloggers.civiblog.org/blog) publish lists of bloggers who have been dooced—or worse—for blogging.

BLOG RULE #28: Blogging can get you fired! Hundreds of employees have been fired, or dooced, for blogging about their employers.

Here are a few high-profile examples of employees who have been dooced for blogging:

• Former Delta Air Lines flight attendant Ellen Simonetti was fired in October 2004 for posting photos of herself, dressed in her company uniform, on her blog, "Diary of a Flight Attendant" (www.queenofsky .net). As reported by USA Today, People magazine, the Associated Press, TheMiamiHerald.com and other national media outlets—and as widely discussed and commented upon in the blogosphere—one photo showed Simonetti with her blouse partly unbuttoned, exposing a bit of bra. In another photo, Simonetti was stretched across a row of plane seats with her skirt somewhat hiked up.

Simonetti filed a sexual discrimination lawsuit in U.S. District Court in Atlanta in September 2005, after being issued a "right to sue" letter from the United States Equal Employment Opportunity Commission. In her suit, Simonetti claims that male employees with potentially insensitive postings on their blogs have gone unpunished by Delta. The case, which "could plow fresh legal ground on whether a company can take action against an employee for operating a blog,"[8] is being closely watched by the legal community, employers, and the blogosphere.

- A southern California auto club fired 27 workers in August 2005 for posting blog comments that were offensive to coworkers. The posts, which were written by the bloggers at home, criticized club members and discussed the employee-bloggers' plans to delay roadside assistance. In addition, the bloggers' posts included comments about the weight and sexual orientation of coworkers. At least one worker is reported to have complained to management about feeling harassed by the offensive blog posts.[9] According to an Automobile Club spokeswoman, "In the tabloid age, people think that they can say what they want. This is not [covered] by free speech . . . you can't just say what you want."[10]

- Jessica Cutler, a twenty-something staff assistant to U.S. Senator Mike DeWine, gained international notoriety and lost her job, thanks to her blog, Washingtonienne, in which she anonymously shared details of her sex life on Capitol Hill. Cutler's blog detailed the peccadilloes of her six sexual partners, including a man who enjoyed spanking and being spanked, along with a married Bush administration official, whom Cutler claims paid her $400 for each lunch-hour tryst. Written anonymously and intended only to amuse herself and her closest girlfriends, Cutler's X-rated blog became big news in Washington, D.C., and around the globe when the popular online gossip site, Wonkette, outed the former Senate staffer's blog.[11]

- Mark Jen lost his job as an associate product manager at Google after commenting about potential future products on his blog, 99zeros .blogspot.com. Jen was later hired by the consumer Internet service Plaxo and helped draft the company's first blog policy. Jen told *USA Today* that he found Google's reaction to his blog "shocking."[12]

- Joe Gordon became the first person in Britain to be fired for blogging about an employer. The eleven-year employee of the Waterstone's bookstore chain in Edinburgh, Scotland, was sacked for writing critical posts in which, for example, he called the company "Bastardstone's" and referred to a supervisor as the "Evil Boss."[13]

- An elementary school teacher in Texas resigned after an investigation revealed that she had used her class computer to access a personal blog, which contained sexually explicit content and disparaging remarks about her students.[14]

- A Boston University instructor was fired for blogging about a "distractingly attractive student."[15]

- A nanny was dismissed from her position for revealing too much about herself and her employers on her blog.[16]

- In 2003, Michael Hanscom, a Microsoft contractor, was fired after posting photos of Apple computers arriving at a Microsoft loading dock.

Because Hanscome's post described a building, Microsoft claimed he had violated security policy.[17]

- Wells Fargo terminated an employee for poking fun at his coworkers on his blog.[18]

Your Personal Blog May Keep You from Getting Hired, Too

If your blog doesn't get you fired from your current job, it just may prevent you from getting hired down the road. According to the Society for Human Resource Management, some employers are taking time to review prospective employees' personal blogs before hiring them.[19]

Not surprising. A personal blog that contains candid photos and revealing comments would certainly give an employer much greater insight into a recruit's true personality and lifestyle than a resume and reference check could ever provide.

Here are four pieces of advice for bloggers who are in the job market:

1. Think twice before you write. A witty comment that scores a laugh with readers today could cost you your dream job tomorrow.
2. Don't list your blog on your resume if there is any chance that any reader for any reason could be offended by or misconstrue the meaning of your content.
3. If you don't want a prospective employer to know about your offbeat hobbies, counterculture lifestyle, political leanings, or personal interests, then don't blog about them.
4. Blog search engines make it easy for prospective and current employers to uncover the blogs of recruits and employees. Before you post, consider whether your beloved blog is worth more than your job and your future.

What's the Lesson for Employers?

As part of the organization's blog-management training program, review with employees the company's code of conduct, ethics policy, sexual harassment and discrimination policy, blog and electronic communications guidelines, and any other employment rules and policies that are in place. Let employees know that a violation of any policy is a violation—regardless of whether it is accomplished on a blog or via another communications tool. Make sure employees understand that policy violations will result in disciplinary action, up to and including termination.

As an added precaution, have each employee sign and date acknowledgment forms confirming that they have read and understand each of the organization's policies and agree to comply with each policy or accept the consequences. In addition, require employees to sign a consent form granting management the right to monitor each employee's business and personal blogs.

In the event of litigation, the organization may need employees' signed and dated acknowledgment and consent forms to demonstrate that the company has adhered to best practices and made every reasonable effort to maintain a civil business environment. Advice to employees: Familiarize yourself with all of your employer's rules and policies before you blog. Do not blog blind.

Recap and Blog Action Plan

1. The biggest risk individual employee-bloggers face is being fired (or *dooced,* in blog parlance) for blog content or usage.
2. If your blog doesn't get you fired from your current job, it may prevent you from getting hired down the road.
3. Think before you post. If there is any chance that your entry might violate an employment policy or code of conduct, or otherwise harm the organization, don't publish it.
4. If you don't want a prospective employer to know about your personal life, then don't blog about it.

CHAPTER 16

EMPLOYEE-BLOGGERS BEWARE 2: BLOGGING CAN GET YOU SUED!

Apple's DNA is innovation, and the protection of our trade secrets is crucial to our success.

—APPLE COMPUTER, INC. ON ITS LAWSUIT AGAINST THINKSECRET.COM, *WASHINGTON POST*[1]

Although there have been just a few lawsuits to date involving blogs, legal experts agree that, given the growing popularity of blogs and the propensity of bloggers to use their sites to opine on people, products, service quality, and businesses in general, the potential for litigation is huge.

It's not just employers with deep pockets who are at risk of litigation. As the cases detailed in this chapter illustrate, individual bloggers—without the financial wherewithal to cover the cost of legal fees or settlements—also may be subject to legal claims based on the contents of their blogs.

BLOG RULE #29: Blogging can get you sued! Given the growing popularity of blogs and the propensity of bloggers to use their sites to opine on people, products, service quality, and businesses, the potential for litigation (aimed at organizations and individuals) is huge.

Real-Life News Site Lawsuit 1: Apple Takes a Bite out of Trade-Secret Theft

In one closely watched case, Apple Computer in January 2005 sued Harvard undergraduate Nicholas M. Ciarelli and his company, The dePlume

Organization LLC, in California Superior Court, accusing him of illegally misappropriating and publishing trade secrets on his Mac news website, Think Secret (www.thinksecret.com). The story of the computer giant's claim against the nineteen-year-old college freshman has been covered by mainstream media outlets, including the *Washington Post,*[2] *InformationWeek,*[3] and the *Village Voice,*[4] as well as numerous blogs and news sites—including ThinkSecret.com, which also makes available court filings related to the litigation for download.

According to media reports, Ciarelli has been operating Think Secret since age 13, when he first began publishing insider news and rumors about Apple. The site, which generates millions of page views per month,[5] features a click-through box that reads "Got Dirt?" and encourages readers to contribute "news tips and insider information" via the site's anonymous voice-mail system or e-mail form.[6]

Apple's suit "alleges that ThinkSecret.com induced tipsters to break non-disclosure agreements."[7] And Ciarelli, who uses the alias Nick dePlume, certainly has scored some scoops. In 2001, ThinkSecret.com was first to report that Apple planned to introduce a G4 version of the PowerBook laptop series. In December 2004, Think Secret accurately predicted the rollout of a new Apple software package and a sub-$500 computer.

After first sending a series of letters warning Ciarelli to stop publishing proprietary information, Apple filed a lawsuit accusing the teen of misappropriating trade secrets on January 4, 2005.[8]

On March 4, 2005, attorney Terry Gross (who agreed to represent Ciarelli and his company on a *pro bono* basis since the teen could not afford to defend himself against a corporation with pockets as deep as Apple's[9]) filed a motion to have the lawsuit dismissed on First Amendment grounds. The motion argues that Think Secret is engaged in journalism and uses news-gathering methods (including accepting news tips from anonymous sources) that are used by traditional journalists. "Under the First Amendment, a journalist cannot be held liable for trade secret misappropriation or inducing breach of contract for publishing newsworthy information lawfully obtained," according to Think Secret's court filings.[10]

The court filings also argue that "the information published is not entitled to trade secret protection under the law as it already had been publicly disclosed and had no economic value in the short time between Think Secret's publication and Apple's press releases"[11] announcing Apple's new software and computer.

InformationWeek notes that "lawyers and academics have weighed in on both sides of the case," with supporters of Apple's position arguing that the Uniform Trade Secrets Act (adopted by about 45 states) could prevent a third party like Think Secret from revealing confidential information that it knowingly receives from people (Apple employees, for example) who are bound by nondisclosure agreements.[12]

Suffolk University Law School professor Andrew Beckerman-Rodau raises a point that is of special significance to all employers operating in the age of the blogs. As Beckerman-Rodau told the *Washington Post*, "This case raises legal and marketing issues for these companies because the providers of this information are their fans, people they don't want to antagonize, even though they may not want these things published right away."[13]

Real-Life Blog Lawsuit 2: Comments Posted by Anonymous Readers Trigger Suit Against Blogger

As reported by the *Wall Street Journal*,[14] Traffic-Power.com, an Internet company, has sued blog operator Aaron Wall for comments that readers posted, often anonymously, to Wall's blog, SEOBook.com.

Traffic-Power.com's suit, which was filed in a Nevada state court in August 2005 then moved to federal district court a month later,[15] alleges that Wall published confidential company information, as well as "false and defamatory information" on his blog. According to published reports, Traffic-Power.com first asked Wall to remove the offending material from his blog, and sued only after Wall refused to do so.[16]

Given the candid, tell-all nature of the blogosphere, it is no surprise that Wall has used his blog to tell the tale of his lawsuit. He has posted the text of the lawsuit on his blog, solicited donations to help cover his legal costs, speculated on which reader comments may have triggered the claim, and kept his readers informed on the status of the case.[17]

According to the *Wall Street Journal*, legal analysts view the suit as a possible test case for determining what protections a blog operator does or doesn't have for allegedly defamatory material that is posted to a site's comments section by others.[18]

Recap and Blog Action Plan

1. Legal experts agree that, given the growing popularity of blogs and the propensity of bloggers to use their sites to opine on people, products, service quality, and businesses, the potential for blog-related litigation is huge. Remember: The easiest way to control electronic risk is to control written content—including readers' comments.

2. In the blogosphere, it's not just deep-pocketed employers who are at risk of litigation. Individual bloggers may also be subject to legal claims based on the contents of their blogs, regardless of their ability to cover the cost of legal counsel or settlements.

3. The easiest way to control blog-related litigation risks is to control written content. If you don't post it, it can't come back to haunt you. Post it, and you create a written business record, which may be used as evidence (for or against your case) should a lawsuit arise.

CHAPTER 17

HOW TO BLOG WITHOUT GETTING FIRED

Eight Tips for Bloggers Who Want to Keep Their Jobs and Stay out of Court

You can write about work, absolutely. Go ahead and vent. But you're taking your livelihood into your hands.

—Dooce.com's Heather Armstrong, quoted in *San Diego Union-Tribune*[1]

Tip 1. Blogging About Your Job or Your Boss May Get You Fired

Employees have been fired for blogging about their employers' people, products, and services. Employees have been fired for posting photos of themselves dressed in their company uniforms while off duty. Employees have been fired for posting embarrassing photos about the goings-on inside companies. Employees have been fired for alerting the blogosphere to what a jerk a particular manager is or what a joke a company's policies and procedures are.

At the end of the day, blogging (negatively or positively) about your job or your boss is likely to get you fired—regardless of whether you blog at home or at the office, with your equipment or the company's, or anonymously or under your own name.

Tip 2. Familiarize Yourself with Your Employer's Policy First; Blog Second

Don't blog until you read (and understand) all of your organization's employment policies, including the organization's blog rules and guidelines. Familiarize yourself with the company's blog rules and policy, electronic communications guidelines, code of conduct, confidentiality rules and policies, sexual harassment and discrimination guidelines, and any other rules and policies your employer may impose. Violation of any employment policy, whether committed on a blog or another electronic communications tool, can get you fired.

As reported by London's *TimesOnline,* a whopping 94 percent of employees in the United Kingdom are unaware of their companies' blogging policies.[2] If you don't know whether your employer has a blog policy that governs both business and personal blogging, be sure to ask first and save the blogging for later.

Tip 3. The First Amendment Does Not Protect Bloggers

Do you believe that the First Amendment grants you the right to say whatever you want on your personal blog? Many U.S. bloggers mistakenly believe that the First Amendment protects their jobs. It doesn't. The First Amendment only restricts government control of speech; it says nothing about private employers. That said, legal experts note that blogging by state or federal employees may be protected by the First Amendment.[3]

BLOG RULE #30: The First Amendment does not protect bloggers.

Tip 4. Employment at Will Means You Can Be Fired for Any Reason—Including Blogging

Do you work in an employment-at-will state? If you do, watch those blog posts! Private employers operating in employment-at-will states are free to fire employees for just about any reason, including blogging, as long as it is not discriminatory or in retaliation for whistle-blowing or union organizing.[4]

Laws prevent employers from terminating employees on the basis of race, ethnicity, sex, age, religion, disability, and sexual orientation in some places. But when it comes to blogging, even keeping your personal blog clean of work-related material won't necessarily protect you from termination.

As attorney Daniel M. Klein of Atlanta-based Buckley & Klein told the *New York Times*: "It doesn't matter if you blog about skydiving or pornography. If your employer feels the blog makes you a poor representative of their corporate values, the executives have the freedom to disassociate themselves from you."[5]

Tip 5. Know the Law: Some Bloggers Have Protections Not Available to At-Will Employees

According to the National Workrights Institute, five states—California, New York, Colorado, Montana, and North Dakota—have recently enacted laws limiting the circumstances under which an employer can fire an employee for an off-duty activity that is not related to the job.[6]

In addition, employee-bloggers in states with anti-SLAPP (Strategic Litigation Against Public Participation) statutes may have some recourse against employers who are found to have "improperly quashed their employees' First Amendment rights" in connection with blog-related activities.[7]

The National Labor Relations Act offers bloggers some protections if they are writing about wages or working conditions. And bloggers who are employed by the government or belong to unions may have some protections not available to at-will employees.

Tip 6. Beware: Employers Are Prescreening Job Applicants' Blogs

The Society for Human Resource Management reports that some employers are taking time to review prospective employees' personal blogs.[8] Blog search engines make it easy for prospective employers to check out job applicants' blogs. Do you really want to give a prospective employer one more reason to reject you? If you're in the job market, consider deactivating your blog or focusing solely on content that is certain to appeal to a prospective employer by highlighting your professional expertise or positioning yourself as a thought leader.

Tip 7. Remember: Anyone Can Read Your Posts—Forever

Thanks to the permalink, a unique web address is created for every posting on a blog. Bloggers link to one another's posts, which typically remain accessible forever via the permalink (unlike web pages, which are subject to change and removal). The permalink creates a double-edged sword for business, giving blogs "a viral quality, so a pertinent post can gain broad attention amazingly fast—and reputations can get taken down just as quickly."[9] For employees, the permalink means that any nasty comments, gossip, rumors, insults, and criticisms you may have posted about your manager or your company are out there in the blogosphere just waiting to be discovered. In other words, an ugly post may not get you fired today, but it could cost you your job a month, year, or decade from now.

Tip 8. Modify or Deactivate Your Comment Function

As a blog publisher, you may one day be held legally responsible for readers' comments. Don't allow your blog to be blindsided. Consider deactivating or modifying the comment feature of your blog, or require readers to register before posting comments. For maximum protection, screen readers' comments pre-post to avoid publishing content that is defamatory or inaccurate, violates copyright law, reveals confidential information, or otherwise is inappropriate, offensive, or in violation of laws, rules, regulations, and policies.

Recap and Blog Action Plan

1. Blogging about your job, boss, or coworkers may get you fired.
2. The First Amendment does not protect bloggers who work for private employers.
3. Employment at will means you can be fired for any reason—including blogging.
4. Know the law. Some bloggers have protections not available to at-will employees.
5. Beware: Some employers screen job applicants' blogs.
6. Thanks to the permalink, your boss can read your posts—forever.
7. Don't post reader comments without first reviewing—and as necessary editing or rejecting—them.

PART 6

PUBLIC RELATIONS IN THE BLOGOSPHERE

Telling Your Story, Recruiting Customer Evangelists, Positioning CEO Bloggers

CHAPTER 18

THE RULES OF ENGAGEMENT HAVE CHANGED

Blogs Make It Harder to Control Your Message and Your Brand

Companies over the past few centuries have gotten used to shaping their message. Now [thanks to blogs] they're losing control of it.

—BusinessWeek[1]

Before blogging, corporate public relations (PR) professionals relied on a fairly standard formula to get the word out about their organizations, to position executives, to promote products, and to sell services.

Specifically, press releases were written and distributed to the mainstream media via snail mail, fax, and in recent years e-mail. Phones were "worked" to build favorable relationships with reporters, editors, and broadcast producers. Business luncheons, golf outings, and other networking events were held to help nurture and grow relationships with customers and key influencers. Speeches were made, board seats were secured, and op-ed columns were written to help position CEOs and senior executives as industry opinion leaders.

In the event of a crisis in the pre-blog era, the PR team would spring into action, relying on the relationships they had nurtured and the goodwill they had built up among the mainstream media to tell the company's side of the story and help manage the disaster. Although a high-profile, newsworthy corporate disaster has never been (and will never be) a day at the beach, in the preblog era, containment was considerably easier than it is today.

Before blogging, there simply were fewer reporters available to share the company's disaster story with the public. Newspaper and television reporters rarely have the opportunity for follow-up coverage. After a story breaks, the mainstream media tend to move on to the next big story. Consequently, with the exception of a few notable cases, most corporate crises in the pre-blog era had a limited media shelf life. After an initial flurry of media coverage, the story would more or less die.

Thanks to Blogs, Business News—Good or Bad—Lives Forever

Thanks to blogs, business news (good or bad) can now be distributed—instantly and globally—by millions of citizen journalists who do not face the same professional and ethical constraints as the mainstream media. Without journalistic reputations and established careers to protect, bloggers are free to (intentionally or unintentionally) publish unsubstantiated rumors, spread lies, defame individuals and organizations, beat the drum for any given issue or cause in which the blogger has a stake, and—in some cases—do irreparable harm to corporate credibility, executive reputations, and investor confidence.

Without the ethical constraints placed on the mainstream media, bloggers are free to accept fees from unscrupulous corporate executives who hire bloggers to bash the competition—with no clear trail back to the sponsoring organization. *Forbes* reports that as many as 60 percent of organized blog attacks are paid for in this manner.[2] Compounding the problem is the fact that the more controversial, outspoken, or ugly a blogger's attack is, the more likely it is that the blogosphere will link to it. The attacker's search engine rating climbs as the corporate reputation tumbles.[3]

Without the benefit of confirmed, reliable sources or experienced fact checkers, bloggers may unintentionally (or intentionally) post content that is inaccurate, incomplete, or downright false.

Without the advice of legal counsel, bloggers might reveal trade secrets, expose confidential company information, or invade personal privacy.

Thanks to incoming links, outgoing links, permalinks, ping services, and syndication, a factually inaccurate or otherwise damaging post can bounce around the Internet from one blog to millions of other blogs forever—archived and ever-accessible to new readers.

With the exception of employees whose business and personal blogging is guided by workplace rules and policies, bloggers for the most part operate unconstrained in the anything-goes, freewheeling culture of the blogosphere. Short on restrictions and long on what often is a misunderstood "right" to free speech, the blogosphere has the potential to become what *Forbes* calls the "ultimate vehicle for brand-bashing, personal attacks, political extremism, and smear campaigns."[4]

> **BLOG RULE #31:** Thanks to incoming links, outgoing links, permalinks, ping services, and syndication, a factually inaccurate or otherwise damaging post can bounce around the Internet from one blog to millions of other blogs forever—archived and ever-accessible to new readers.

Journalists Rely on Blogs for Stories and Sources

In spite of the potential downsides, PR professionals cannot afford to turn their backs on the blogosphere. When it comes to media relations, for example, organizations that are not yet blogging are missing out on an important opportunity to communicate with print, broadcast, and online reporters who rely on blogs for business news.

More than half (51 percent) of journalists surveyed report using blogs regularly, with 28 percent relying on blogs for their daily reporting. Among the journalists who use blogs, 70 percent say they turn to blogs to locate story ideas, conduct research, reference facts, find sources, and uncover breaking news, according to the Annual Euro RSCG Magnet and Columbia University Survey.[5]

The public is increasingly going online for news, too. According to London's *TimesOnline*, a Carnegie Corporation study reveals that the web is increasingly the choice for news among 18-to-34-year-olds. Forty-four percent of survey respondents read news online at least once a day, versus 19 percent who read a printed newspaper daily.[6]

Public Relations Must Adapt and Change—or Suffer the Consequences

Although 62 percent of Internet users may not know what a blog is,[7] there is no question that blogs are rapidly—and forever—changing the way PR people and media relations professionals do business. Among the professional communicators surveyed by Edelman in 2005, more than 80 percent said that they know what a blog is, compared with 60 percent just 12 months earlier.[8] And more than 60 percent of organizations surveyed by iUpload and Guidewire Group report that they are now using external blogs for public relations and marketing purposes.[9]

> **BLOG RULE #32**: Blogs are rapidly—and forever—changing the way PR people and media relations professionals do business.

Bloggers Move to the Top of Corporate Media Lists

Public relations/media relations professionals can no longer afford to rely solely on the traditional mainstream media to communicate the organization's message in a crisis—or any other time, for that matter. Today, influential bloggers must be added to the PR professional's electronic address book, right along with mainstream reporters, editors, and broadcast news producers.

Until now, identifying influential bloggers has not been quite as easy as developing a traditional media list. Although there are numerous mainstream media directories on the market, in which journalists' contact information and pitch preferences are published, until this point PR people for the most part have had to track down influential bloggers on their own. Given the extra work involved in identifying "the right" bloggers, it's no surprise that 48 percent of bloggers report that they have never been contacted by companies or their public relations representatives.[10]

Not surprisingly, change is coming. *Bacon's Information*, long a source of up-to-date media data for PR professionals, began compiling a blog database in fall 2005.[11] Ideally, that directory—and others that are sure to follow—will help facilitate the all-important job of identifying, contacting, and growing relationships with journalists and other influential bloggers who can help (or hurt) the organization as it navigates the blogosphere.

Short of using *Bacon's* or some other media directory that lists bloggers' *beats*—the industries and companies that bloggers follow and write about—PR people are advised to act immediately to identify, contact, and start building mutually beneficial relationships with influential bloggers in your organization's "space." A few tips:

- Visit blogs operated by your organization's employees, competitors, industry associations, critics, and fans.
- Use blog search engines to monitor the blogosphere on an ongoing basis. At any given time, you should know exactly who is saying

what about your company, industry, executives, products, and competitors.

- Follow links from one posting to another. Visit sites listed on influencers' "blogrolls," or lists of links to external sites favored or recommended by the blogger.
- Subscribe to blogs operated by influencers, critics, and supporters.
- Track the media coverage that is generated by influential bloggers.

The goal of all this blogosphere research is to determine the following:

- Which bloggers are most influential among your organization's target audiences of customers and prospects, employees and recruits, mainstream and online media, other bloggers, government officials, and so on?
- Who has posted positive comments about your organization in the past?
- Who in the past has been critical of your organization, products, or customer service?
- Which bloggers have expressed opposition to, or support of, your industry as a whole?
- Who among your employees is blogging?
- What type of content do your employees' personal blogs focus on?
- Have any of your employees established a position as an influential blogger with a large number of incoming and outgoing links and a high search engine ranking?
- Are your employee-bloggers capable of walking the fine line between honesty and corporate evangelism? You don't want to drive away readers with company propaganda, but you do want to tap into your employees' readership base.
- Who is blogging about your organization's competitors?
- Which bloggers could most likely help (or hurt) your organization in the event of a major "we're going to get your company" blogstorm?
- Does your organization have any blogging "superfans" who could be recruited as customer evangelists or *brand bloggers* to help spread the good word about your company, products, people, and plans?

Armed with that type of information, your organization will be well positioned to develop and implement public relations, media relations, marketing, and perhaps advertising strategies and activities designed to communicate effectively with influential bloggers, their readers, and the mainstream media who follow them.

Recap and Blog Action Plan

1. Thanks to blogs, business news can be distributed—instantly and globally—by millions of bloggers.
2. Without journalistic reputations or careers to protect, bloggers are free to print (intentionally or unintentionally) unsubstantiated rumors, lies, and defamatory remarks, and can generally beat the drum for any given issue or cause in which they have a stake.
3. Bloggers are free to accept fees from unscrupulous corporate executives who hire them to bash the competition. *Forbes* reports that as many as 60 percent of blog attacks are paid for in this manner.[12]
4. Fifty-one percent of journalists use blogs regularly, with 28 percent relying on blogs for their daily reporting. Of journalists who use blogs, 70 percent turn to blogs to locate story ideas, conduct research and reference facts, find sources, and uncover breaking news.[13]
5. PR professionals must act now to identify and establish relationships with influential bloggers, including "superfans" who could be recruited as customer evangelists.

SPREADING THE WORD AND SELLING THE BRAND THROUGH CUSTOMER EVANGELISTS AND BRAND BLOGGERS

The blog is the best relationship generator you've ever seen.

—ROBERT SCOBLE, MICROSOFT TECHNICAL EVANGELIST AND PUBLISHER, SCOBLEIZER.COM[1]

As reported by *Ad Age*, McDonald's in 2004 announced that it was adopting a new marketing technique called *brand journalism*. The concept calls for the telling of many different stories to many different audiences, rather than using one universal message to reach everyone.

As the fast-food giant's chief marketing officer, Larry Light, told *Ad Age*, brand journalism is a "brand narrative or brand chronicle." It is a way to record "what happens to a brand in the world," and create ad communications to tell the whole story of a brand over time.[2]

Sounds a lot like business blogging, doesn't it? Multiple writers with varied perspectives and unique voices use external blogs to tell the organization's diverse stories (along with their own personal tales, in some cases) to their own audiences (large and small) of blog readers and fans.

For example, the organization's human resources director could blog about the challenges of recruiting and retaining talented employees (and in the process subtly position the company as a desirable place to work). The IT director could write about emerging technologies and their potential impact on global business communications over the next decade (and thus communicate the fact that the company employs some of the brightest visionaries in the industry). The CEO could blog about the need for the nation's business leaders to work together to eradicate adult illiteracy (and thereby position the organization as a concerned corporate citizen whose CEO is also attuned to social issues that go beyond an emphasis merely on the bottom line).

At the end of the day, an organization that puts employees to work blogging externally is using a form of brand journalism to communicate a number of equally important messages to a diverse group of equally important audiences. That is a feat that no brochure, no advertisement, no press release, and no promotional event could accomplish on its own. That is the power of the business blog.

Singing the Praises of Customer Evangelists

In addition to using employee- and executive-bloggers to tell the organization's various stories, many organizations are turning to *corporate evangelism* as a means to get the blogosphere buzzing. In a comprehensive article on corporate evangelism, *U.S. News & World Report* explains that "the goal is to find and identify those customers who are already crazy about your product or service—who are actively talking it up in blogs or web forums, for instance—and turning them with loads of personal attention into 'customer evangelists' who then spread the word to others."[3] In other words, customer evangelists are *superfans* whom "the rest of us seek out and trust for advice about what cars, computers, and clothing to buy."[4]

The facts certainly support the premise behind customer evangelism. "Regular people" (including superfans and nonexecutive employee-bloggers) are viewed as three times more believable than established authority figures, according to an Edelman study.[5] According to another recent survey, one-third of all consumers would prefer to receive product information from friends and specialists, as opposed to getting it from advertisers.[6]

Vespa Scoots Through the Blogosphere with Customer Evangelists

U.S. News & World Report cites Vespa, the Italian motor scooter company, as one organization that has turned to bloggers as customer evangelists. Vespa in 2005 retained two superfans to blog on the company's site about the pleasures of scootering. In exchange for sharing stories about their passion for scootering, the two superfan-bloggers get the opportunity to test-drive new Vespa models and take home seat covers, rain jackets, and other Vespa tchotchkes.[7]

Customer evangelists are defined as real people giving testimony about a product and a company they feel genuinely passionate about. How passionate are Vespa's superfan-bloggers? "My agenda is to get more people scootering and get more people to buy Vespa," is what one of the bloggers told *U.S. News & World Report*.[8] Spoken like a passionate superfan.

Putting the Power of Brand Blogging to Work

One step beyond customer evangelists are *brand bloggers*,[9] "fanatics" who are devoted to writing about their favorite brands on their own dedicated blogs, at their own expense, on their own time. Brand bloggers devote themselves to writing—mainly positively, but occasionally negatively—about the brands they feel passionately about. "For these bloggers, intertwining their personal stories and commentaries gives them a stake in defining the brand's image while linking them with fans of similar mind across the country," the *New York Times* reports.[10]

Do a quick Google search, and you'll finds brand bloggers with sites dedicated to McDonald's (see McChronicles at http://mcchronicles.blog spot.com),[11] Weight Watchers, LEGO, Apple, TiVo, and Harley-Davidson,[12] among other familiar and not-so-familiar brands.

Consider, for example, brand blogger Michael Marx, whose site, the barqsman.com, is devoted entirely to Barq's root beer. A Barq's drinker for fifteen years, Marx refers to the brand as "my beer." His dedicated blog, which features Marx's affectionate musings about Barq's, comments from fellow Barq's fans, Barq's commercials, and other Barq's news, was featured in the *New York Times* in 2005 as part of a story on brand blogs.[13] Barq's received a million dollars' worth of national publicity free—courtesy of one root beer–loving brand blogger!

Understandably, some organizations are concerned about losing control of the brand message as it moves away from the company's communications team and into the hands of brand bloggers and customer evangelists. That fear may be particularly valid for organizations that fail to engage their devoted brand bloggers. For example, the *New York Times* reports that Coca-Cola, which owns Barq's, was unaware of Marx's blog when contacted by the reporter for comments.[14]

BLOG RULE #33: It pays to put customer evangelists and brand bloggers to work creating buzz in the blogosphere.

Influential Friends Can Translate into Sales at the Cash Register

In addition to customer evangelists and brand bloggers, it pays to have influential friends in the blogosphere. Take, for example, the case of entrepreneur Shayne McQuade, inventor of the Voltaic Backpack, which is designed to keep the electronic gadgets of hikers and travelers charged via built-in solar panels. As reported by *Fortune*, McQuade solicited a blogger friend to mention the Voltaic Backpack on his environmentally friendly blog, Treehugger. Within hours of Treehugger's mention, the Voltaic Backpack was being talked about in other popular blogs, resulting in a "flurry of orders."[15]

McQuade told *Fortune*, "Overnight what was supposed to be laying a little groundwork became my launch. This is the ultimate word-of-mouth marketing channel."[16] Indeed.

Marqui's Paybloggers Program

Short on customer evangelists, brand bloggers, or influential friends who are willing to write about your company and products purely out of a sense of passion, brand loyalty, or personal friendship? No problem. One guaranteed way to get bloggers to write about your organization, and thereby generate buzz in the blogosphere, is to pay them to do so.

Software firm Marqui pioneered this controversial approach when it launched its highly successful "Paybloggers Program" in December 2004. As detailed on the company's website, www.marqui.com, and reported by *Forbes* and *BusinessWeek,* Marqui signed twenty bloggers to three-month contracts, paying each blogger $800 per month to write (positively or negatively) about the company on a weekly basis. In an effort to avoid a backlash, Marqui required its twenty paid bloggers to display a logo on their sites, disclosing the fact that they were receiving payments from the company in exchange for their Marqui-related posts.

Marqui reports that it invested $200,000 over the first six months of the program.[17] Although the Paybloggers Program triggered an ethical debate in the blogosphere, the company credits the blog program with generating a number of positive results:

- Marqui's Google results grew exponentially, from 2,040 to 278,000 in just two weeks.
- The number of unique visitors to Marqui's website jumped to 150,000 in one month.
- The Paybloggers Program generated more than 100 press clips from respected national publications, including *Forbes* and *Business-Week*.
- Marqui's CEO was nominated for *Fast Company's* 2005 Fast 50.
- The company won the 2005 InnoTech Innovation Award.
- Marqui experienced a notable increase in inbound leads, with the company's customer acquisition rate growing by 43 percent a quarter.[18]

Is a *paid evangelist* program right for your organization? Consider three questions before making up your mind:

1. Is there any possibility that a fee-based blog-evangelist program could backfire on your organization, negatively affecting consumer trust or product sales?
2. Would the negative comments generated by an outraged blogosphere negate any positives your paid evangelists might generate?
3. Short of cash, is there anything else that your organization could offer influential bloggers to encourage them to take a close look at your organization and perhaps write about your products or services? According to the 2005 blogger survey from Edelman and Technorati, fully 70 percent of bloggers would appreciate receiving product samples to evaluate on their blogs.[19] Perhaps this would be a better alternative—less expensive to the company and less offensive to the blogosphere—than cash payments.

Recap and Blog Action Plan

1. External blogging is a form of brand journalism that enables the company to communicate several equally important messages to a diverse group of equally important audiences. That is the power of the business blog.

2. Corporate evangelism, customer evangelism, and brand blogging work, in part, because consumers find "regular people" three times more credible than established authority figures.
3. Influential friends in the blogosphere can have an enormous impact on an organization's brand positioning, marketing, and sales.
4. One guaranteed way to get bloggers to write about your organization, and thereby generate buzz in the blogosphere, is to pay them to do so.
5. Consider the risks before embarking on a paid evangelist program.

CHAPTER 20

POSITIONING THE CEO-BLOGGER AS OPINION LEADER

If you want to lead, blog.

—Jonathan Schwartz, President and COO, Sun Microsystems, quoted in *Harvard Business Review*[1]

Given that corporate reputations are in part defined by the chief executive officer,[2] it should come as no surprise that blogging by CEOs and other C-level executives is on the rise. The number of CEOs blogging rose significantly between 2004 and 2005, up from zero to 18 percent in just 12 months, according to a study from Edelman.[3] Heeding the advice of experts who recommend that chief executives engage more intimately with a broad range of internal and external stakeholders,[4] more than 30 percent of CEOs and senior managers who currently blog are doing so externally.[5]

Writing in the *Harvard Business Review*, Sun Microsystems President and COO Jonathan Schwartz predicts that "in ten years, most of us will communicate directly with customers, employees, and the broader business community through blogs." And he puts his C-level peers on notice that they had better become part of the two-way conversation of the blogosphere, or risk having outsiders speak for their companies.[6]

BLOG RULE #34: Blogging by CEOs and other C-level executives who want to engage internal and external stakeholders is on the rise.

Look Who's Blogging

Among the organizations with CEOs and executives who have already jumped into the blogosphere are Edelman, Sun Microsystems, Jupitermedia,[7] Boeing, Disney's ABC Cable Networks Group, GM, and the Dallas Mavericks, to name only a few.[8]

Winning Over Critics with CEO Candor

Schwartz, writing in the *Harvard Business Review,* said, "Your market and your employees are clamoring for executive engagement and insight. They will value and remember your candor. And you'll be surprised how much you can learn from them."[9]

What follows is an example of a CEO who did in fact use his blog to engage—quite successfully—with one unhappy and vocal prospect. In the process, the CEO not only won over that prospective customer, but doubtless impressed many other customers, prospects, and readers who were wowed by the chief executive's responsiveness and candor.

Real-life scenario: Robin Hopper, president and CEO of iUpload, operates an external blog called iUpload InSights (http://hopper.iupload .com) which is available publicly to customers, prospects, and other third-party readers.

In a post entitled "Lead Management 101," Hopper shared the complaints of one prospective customer. More significantly, Hopper's post revealed how the CEO jumped in personally to connect with the prospect, address admitted communications snafus, and correct a few real problems that the prospect had identified.

By taking a candid, straightforward, can-do approach to the prospect's critical post, Hopper succeeded in establishing iUpload as a reliable brand with a trustworthy, hands-on CEO. To quote a line from the prospect's follow-up comment to Hopper's post: "Well done, iUpload!"

In the interest of privacy, the author of *Blog Rules* has changed the prospect's name to "Mr. X." Otherwise, the CEO's post—and the prospective customer's response—appear as originally written.

Lead Management 101

Mr. X, a potential iUpload customer, was kind enough to email me a heads up on a post he was making to his blog where he was calling iUpload to task on how we handled him as a prospect. Mr. X makes a number of good points in terms of how to manage leads—ones that we try to follow—but obviously we dropped the ball in his case.

Having had a chance to review his post and the supporting records (emails, tasks, etc.) in our CRM package, I did want to share some details from our end.

First, Mr. X asks why executives were involved in his inquiry. iUpload is a small company (20 people) that is growing fast and, especially since our launch at DEMO@15, we have been inundated with product inquiries. We understand the need to respond quickly to each request so everybody here "sells," and we don't apologize for an executive team prepared to roll up their sleeves and be involved in helping customers meet their requirements.

Second, upon review it's fairly apparent that several of Mr. X's points can simply be attributed to email not conveying the intent that a live conversation would have. For example:

- Mr. X mentions that we suggested he come to our office for a meeting. Actually the intent was a phone meeting, not to have him make the trek to Burlington. The vast majority of our clients are in the U.S. and over the course of a year, we might have a half dozen customers/prospects meet with us at our office. The "meeting" suggested in our email was intended to be a phone meeting and that should have been clearer in our email.

- Mr. X references the suggestion that he talk to our VP Strategy as "polite brush-off". Again certainly not the intent of the email, in fact quite the opposite . . . In a conversation surrounding the emails we thought the offer to talk with our VP Strategy might help crystallize how he might use the technology. As many of you know, there is no such thing as a quick sales cycle here, content management and large blogging communities are scoped out and decided on over a period of months so we often get involved in more strategy type sessions as people move through their decision process.

- Third, Mr. X mentions that no one has contacted him since and while I don't dispute that, there is a follow up email logged on our CRM trying to arrange that phone meeting in question that obviously didn't make its way to him. We definitely dropped the ball here, the email should have escalated to a phone follow up.

Thanks again for the note Mr. X, here are just a few of the things you'll see from us as (to steal your term) "Lessons Learned":

- We'll make sure all staff aren't shy about sharing our pricing model. Community Publisher for example starts at $1,000/mth for the full platform with administration, editorial tools, ad-serving capabilities, etc. with incremental charges depending on the number of branded blogs you wish to roll out. We are getting closer to releasing paid for versions of Personal Publisher and as it launches, there is an accompanying pricing section coming to our website.
- We'll do more to promote the fact that we do conduct weekly webinars that are intended to be introductions to our product line to our prospects.
- We'll make sure we're much clearer in emails . . . things like "meeting" meaning a phone/web meeting have just become part of our language here and we need to do a better job of conveying steps that we typically take prospects through to see if there's a fit.

Comments |
Posted By: Mr. X

Comment: I have to admit that after notifying Robin Hopper of my post I was half-expecting that my blog's switch would be flipped to the off position. Since my intent was to help rather than offend I offered to take the post down once he had a chance to review it. This is where it gets good: not only did he not want me to delete this post, Robin told me that he appreciated the feedback, and that he wanted to post something on his blog with a trackback to it! Today, I heard from iUpload. Turns out they weren't trying to brush me off, I just got lost in the middle of a frenetic growth stage and misread their actions. We all make mistakes. If you're good, you fix them. If you're really good you fix the mistakes and then fix the procedures that didn't work. But if you're destined for greatness, you have the guts to let someone like me tell the world what you learned from it. Well done, iUpload![10]

Don't Let the CEO Blog You out of Business

Schwartz cautions C-level executives that "it's riskier not to have a blog" than to "have blogs that can be read by anyone, anywhere in the world."[11] That is not necessarily true.

As numerous high-profile, headline-making e-mail gaffes have demonstrated, the CEO is as capable as any other employee of writing ill-conceived or otherwise disastrous electronic content. Unfortunately, the CEO's inappropriate blog post is more likely to shine a negative light on the organization than is a post written by any other employee. A CEO's offensive or thoughtless blog post has the potential to undermine the investment community's confidence in the organization's leadership, trigger a slide in the company's stock valuation, generate ugly headlines worldwide, and permanently damage the organization's reputation and credibility—just to name a few risks.

How dangerous can the CEO's electronic communications be? Consider these cautionary tales involving CEO blog posts and e-mail.

• Intel CEO Paul Otellini operates an internal blog, which resides behind the company firewall and is intended for employees' eyes only. Otellini discusses Intel business, industry trends, and competitors on his internal blog. Although Otellini does not share the contents of his blog with outsiders, that has not stopped posts from making their way out of the Intel system and into public view[12]—just like confidential company e-mail that (accidentally or intentionally) lands in the in-boxes of reporters who are only too happy to expose executive e-mail gaffes and air the corporation's electronic dirty laundry.

As reported by Edelman and Intelliseek, one potentially embarrassing Otellini post that made its way into the blogosphere in January 2005 read, "While I hate losing share, the reality is that our competitor has a very strong product offering."[13] Not necessarily reassuring news to the investment community.

• Speaking of bad news for investors . . . When the CEO of Cerner Corporation opted to use e-mail to express his displeasure over employee performance, he hoped to motivate his 400 managers to act. They acted all right, posting the CEO's angry message on Yahoo!®, where it was read by an unanticipated audience of 3,100 Cerner employees, as well as financial analysts, investors, and Yahoo subscribers. The result: Cerner's stock valuation, which was $1.5 billion the day the CEO's angry e-mail was sent, plummeted 22 percent, from $44 to $34 per share in just three days.[14]

- Boeing's former president and CEO, Harry Stonecipher, lost his job, damaged his reputation, generated unwanted international news coverage, and created a public relations nightmare for Boeing when e-mail records revealed that he had been having a consensual extramarital affair with a female Boeing executive—and using the company's e-mail system to send her "graphic" electronic love notes. Stonecipher was forced to resign, in part because his indiscretion violated the company's code of conduct, undercutting Stonecipher's credibility as the company's chief ethics enforcer and placing Boeing in a "potentially embarrassing and damaging situation."[15]

There's No Taking Your Words Back Once They're in the Blogosphere

As stated chapters 6, 8, 9, and 10, inappropriate content is inappropriate content, whether it's transmitted via e-mail or posted (and permalinked) on a blog. The primary difference is that risky blog content has a never-ending "viral" quality. You can count on a juicy, salacious, or otherwise unprofessional and embarrassing blog post to be read, linked to, pinged, permalinked, and commented upon by countless readers for years to come.

There is no such thing as 100 percent security or privacy in cyberspace. You cannot rely on confidential internal blog posts to stay safely inside the firewall. You cannot assume that all employees will comply with confidentiality rules and keep internal posts private. Just like confidential company e-mail, sensitive internal blog posts occasionally will make their way out of the organization and into the blogosphere—accidentally or intentionally.

At the end of the day, blogs and e-mail may not be the best ways to communicate confidential, potentially embarrassing, or otherwise damaging information to employees and other insiders. If you don't want to risk having sensitive subject matter exposed to the blogosphere, opt for a face-to-face meeting or a phone call instead. Blogs, like all electronic communications tools, produce written business records. There simply is no taking your words back once your blog post goes live.

> **BLOG RULE #35:** Blogging may not be the best way for CEOs to communicate confidential, potentially embarrassing, or otherwise damaging information to employees and other insiders. There simply is no taking your words back once your blog post goes live.

Self-Assessment for CEO Bloggers

Considering a blog for your CEO or C-level executives? Carefully weigh the potential benefits against the very real risks before proceeding. Here are a few questions to consider before launching a CEO blog.

Is the CEO Prepared to Make the Necessary Time Commitment?

To be a success, a CEO-blogger must spend time researching and writing posts, as well as reviewing and responding to readers' comments and e-mails. According to the Cymfony white paper, "Blogging and Its Impact on Corporate Reputation," General Motors' Vice Chairman Bob Lutz's blog, Fast Lane (fastlane.gmblogs.com), averages 4,000 to 5,000 visits daily and generates 60 to 100 comments per post.[16] That is a lot of consumer commentary to absorb and, as appropriate, reply to via blog or e-mail.

A few extremely popular top-ranked "celebrity" bloggers have already found themselves so overwhelmed by reader e-mail that they have announced plans to curtail their blogging. Although it may be fine for an individual blogger to take a break, consumers may not be so forgiving of a CEO who begins, and then abruptly stops, blogging.

The CEO is the face of the company. The CEO does not have the luxury of ignoring readers' comments or e-mail. Before embarking on a C-level blogging program, make sure senior management understands, and is prepared for, the time-consuming demands of blogging.

Does the CEO Possess an Opinion Maker's Passion and Point of View?

More than one-third of bloggers surveyed (34 percent) blog primarily to gain visibility as authorities or opinion makers within their respective fields, according to Edelman and Technorati.[17] Thanks to blogs, "employees at all levels have found themselves in powerful positions . . . and have found that people are listening to what they say."[18]

What's it take for the CEO to become an opinion maker, a recognized and sought-after expert within the industry and the business community as a whole? First, it takes passion—genuine passion for a specific cause. It also takes a confirmed point of view and the courage to express that viewpoint, regardless of how controversial it may be.

CEOs who are used to having their words "spun" by PR professionals and vetted by lawyers may not be comfortable in the very opinionated culture of the blogosphere.

Is the CEO Willing to Stay the Course and Build Readership Slowly Over Time?

Only 25 percent of U.S. opinion leaders surveyed feel that CEOs make credible information sources.[19] That said, building readerships may be a long, slow process for some CEO-bloggers. Would your CEO be willing to stay the course and continue blogging in spite of a limited audience? Or does the chief executive expect to attract readers numbering in the thousands, tens of thousands, or hundreds of thousands right from the start? Rein in unreasonable expectations, and do not introduce a CEO blog unless the chief executive is committed to a long-term effort.

Does the CEO Enjoy Writing?

The CEO doesn't need to be the best writer in the blogosphere in order to succeed, but it certainly would help if the chief executive enjoyed writing enough to create new posts on a regular basis (at least once a week). Writing for the blog requires honesty, humor, and a willingness to let the writer's genuine personality shine through. Some CEOs may be naturals at writing in the relaxed, conversational, first-person style of the blogosphere. Chief executives who are more comfortable keeping outsiders at arm's length may be unsettled by the candid, confessional writing style that blogging calls for.

Does the CEO Have a Thick Skin?

If you ask for reader comments, you will get comments. And they will not all be positive or flattering. Many will be critical of the company and its products. Some will be downright nasty. Is the CEO's skin thick enough to handle criticisms and complaints from readers? Does the CEO have the patience and personality necessary to treat all readers with respect—no matter how unpleasant or ugly their comments may be? CEOs who are committed to engaging customers and other influencers in the blogosphere should have little problem interacting with and responding to readers' comments and e-mails. Chief executives who are more comfortable with layers of vice presidents standing between the consumer and the CEO are less likely to appreciate the power inherent in the open, two-way conversation of the blogosphere.

Who Will Screen the CEO's Entries and Readers' Comments Pre-Post?

Organizations that want to limit the likelihood of litigation, negative publicity, and other blog-related risks are advised to have the organization's lawyer, compliance officer, or blog czar screen both the CEO's blog entries and readers' comments prior to posting. Although blog enthusiasts recoil at the idea of screening and editing content pre-post, doing so is in the best interest of the organization, its assets, and future. To post unscreened, unedited blog content (the CEO's or other bloggers' for that matter) is simply a bad business practice.

Has the CEO Completed Blog Policy Training?

Best practices call for one corporate blog policy with which all employees (including the CEO) must comply. When it comes to policy and procedures, the CEO should be treated like all other employees. Before starting to blog, the chief executive should participate in formal blog policy training that includes a thorough review of the risks, rules, policies, and procedures associated with business blogging. Require the CEO to sign and date an acknowledgment form, confirming that the chief executive has read, understands, and agrees to comply with the organization's blog policy. If the CEO violates blog policy, the company should follow Boeing's lead and discipline the chief executive immediately—just as it would any other employee-blogger who fails to comply with policy.

Recap and Blog Action Plan

1. Blogging by CEOs and other C-level executives is on the rise, reflecting a desire to engage internal and external audiences.
2. A CEO's inappropriate blog post has the potential to undermine the investment community's confidence in an organization's leadership, trigger a slide in the company's stock valuation, generate ugly headlines worldwide, and damage the organization's reputation and credibility—just to name a few risks.
3. Blogging may not be the best way for CEOs to communicate confidential, potentially embarrassing, or otherwise damaging information to employees and other insiders. There simply is no taking your words back once a blog post goes live.
4. Before staring a CEO blog, carefully weigh the potential benefits against the very real risks.

PART 7

MANAGING YOUR REPUTATION IN THE BLOGOSPHERE

CHAPTER 21

YOU'VE BEEN BLOGGED

How to Prepare for—and Respond to—
An Attack in the Blogosphere

Every company should have someone put into Google the name of the
company or the brand, followed by the word 'sucks.'

—JEFF JARVIS, BUZZMACHINE BLOGGER AND NEWS MEDIA PROFESSIONAL,
QUOTED IN *FORTUNE*[1]

Any organization or individual who has suffered through a bashing in the
blogosphere would agree with *Forbes* reporter Daniel Lyons's assessment
that blogs can be "the ultimate vehicle for brand-bashing, personal attacks,
political extremism, and smear campaigns."[2] What makes the blog such an
effective weapon?

Recipe for Online Destruction

The following list lays out the primary reasons why blogs can be so destruc-
tive:

•   Attacks are sometimes launched by anonymous bloggers who are
not easily identified or fought.
•   With only 4 percent of major U.S. companies operating external
blogs,[3] it's a safe bet that the majority of organizations are woefully ill-
prepared to respond to a blog bashing in an effective or timely fashion. In

fact, the phrase "deer caught in the headlights" comes to mind when imagining how many corporate PR departments, unschooled in blogging culture, would react to an all-out assault in the blogosphere.

- Approximately 50 to 60 percent of blog attacks are sponsored by competitors who use blogs as weapons to unleash hordes of critics on their business rivals, according to one legal expert.[4] Corporate-sponsored attack bloggers not only have a financial incentive to post dirt, but they also might be less likely than individual bloggers to respond to the threat of a lawsuit.

- Under the Communications Decency Act of 1996, blog hosts, as neutral carriers of Internet content, are protected from liability for anything posted on the blogs they host.[5] With no fear of litigation, deep-pocketed blog hosts have little incentive to ensure that bloggers' posts are true, accurate, and fair.

- Unlike reporters who rely on multiple sources and fact-checkers to get the story straight and protect their professional reputations in the process, bloggers have little to lose if they post inaccurate information or spread outright lies. No matter how egregious the error, a blogger may simply remove a damaging post (if threatened with a lawsuit) or just move on to the next day's post—with no loss of reputation or readership.

- Thanks to the permalink and syndication, rumors, lies, gossip, and defamatory remarks can remain archived and accessible forever—long after an organization has countered the attack bloggers' claims online, enlisted the support of the mainstream media, and otherwise done everything possible to communicate its side of the story to set the record straight.

- Only 6 percent of bloggers say they would completely remove a post that contained factually incorrect information about a product or company. That's bad news for business. The good news: Most bloggers would take some action to correct a factual error, including striking through the error and correcting the post (39 percent); creating a new post with new information (25 percent); leaving the error and adding a correction (24 percent); leaving the error and relying on reader comments to correct it (5 percent).[6]

Is your organization capable of responding quickly when bloggers make factual errors or otherwise post "wrong" information about your company? Fully 65 percent of bloggers say e-mail is the best way for an organization to make contact and report an erroneous post.[7] To minimize damage and reduce the number of links to an erroneous post, be sure to contact the blogger as soon as you become aware of an error.

BLOG RULE #36: Blogs are a phenomenal vehicle for attacking companies, brands, and individuals. Be proactive. Prepare today for the blog attack that is likely to hit tomorrow.

Real-Life Blog Disaster Story: Bloggers Put a Lock on Kryptonite

Kryptonite, the manufacturer of the most recognized brand of bicycle locks on the market, suffered a reported $10 million loss and a severely tarnished reputation, following a ten-day blogstorm that took place in September 2004.

As reported by mainstream media outlets including the *New York Times,*[8] *Fortune,*[9] and *Forbes,*[10] as well as bicycling enthusiasts throughout the blogosphere, Kryptonite's troubles started on September 12, when a lone biker used bikeforums.net, a group discussion site (not a blog), to alert bicycle enthusiasts that many of the most expensive and common U-shaped bicycle locks, including some Krypotonite models, could be easily picked with a Bic ballpoint pen. Some 170,000 bikers saw the bikeforums.net posting, according to the *New York Times,* resulting in "full-fledged panic" among bike owners, particularly in New York City, where commuters rely on bikes to get to and from work, couriers use bikes on the job, and "thousands of bikes are stolen each year."[11]

Perhaps because Kryptonite is the leading brand of bike lock, or maybe because the company takes its name from the only substance that can defeat Superman, the blogosphere and mainstream media chose to point the blame at Kryptonite—even though competitors' U-shaped locks were equally vulnerable.[12] Two days after the original post, on September 14, the consumer electronics blog Engadget.com joined numerous other blogs in posting a homemade video demonstrating how to pop open a Kryptonite lock with a Bic pen. Shocked and scared biker-bloggers ramped up their posts and comments.

When the *New York Times* and Associated Press jumped into the act, reporting the story on September 17, their articles set off yet another wave of blogging.[13] As if that were not bad enough, the *New York Times* and other media outlets ran what Kryptonite classifies as a "how to steal a bike article," complete with pictures illustrating how to pop a Kryptonite lock with a Bic pen.[14]

By September 19, just seven days after the original posting, some 1.8

million people had read angry blog postings about Kryptonite and viewed unsettling blog videos demonstrating how easily the locks could be popped, according to blog search engine Technorati.[15]

Compounding Kryptonite's problems: Not all of the information posted by bloggers was true. As *Forbes* pointed out in a November 2005 cover story labeling blogs a "virulent" form of "bash-the-company Web sites,"[16] anti-Kryptonite bloggers spread bogus information, including false claims that all Kryptonite models could be opened with a Bic pen (in truth, only models with a tubular cylinder lock were vulnerable); that Kryptonite was the only brand that had this vulnerability (actually all manufacturers of tubular cylinder locks were affected); and that the company was aware of the problem and chose to conceal it (in reality, Kryptonite developed and implemented a strategic crisis response plan that included the replacement of 380,000 locks).[17]

According to the *New York Times*, as word of Kryptonite's vulnerability spread, cyclists found alternative means of transportation, bicycle shops nationwide pulled the locks off their shelves, and some bike shops even began recommending that bikers replace their $90 U-shaped bicycle locks with sturdy $20 padlocks, available at any hardware store.[18]

How did Kryptonite respond to its flogging in the blogosphere? According to marketing blogs and the mainstream media outlets that relied on those blogs for information, not very well. *Fortune*, for example, criticized Kryptonite for issuing a "bland statement" on September 16, assuring customers that the locks remained a "deterrent to theft" and promising that a new line would be "tougher."[19] In the same article, *Fortune* reported that Kryptonite planned to distribute more than 100,000 free locks as part of its postcrisis lock exchange program, at an estimated cost of $10 million, a sizable chunk of Kryptonite's estimated revenues of $25 million.[20] In fact, by the time the dust settled, Kryptonite would distribute 380,000 locks over a 10-month period.[21]

Kryptonite Mounts a Traditional Response to a Nontraditional Bashing

In spite of the bashing Kryptonite took in the blogosphere (from marketing blogs in particular) and regardless of the misinformation that continues to circulate in the blogosphere and mainstream business media, the company argues that it did in fact respond to the crisis in a strategic and appropriate fashion, given Kryptonite's industry (manufacturing) and limited resources (25 total employees).[22]

Unfortunately, because Kryptonite chose to communicate its response through the traditional mainstream media and to ignore influential critics in the blogosphere altogether, its response was deemed inadequate and roundly (and loudly) criticized by influential marketing bloggers, as well as some mainstream media outlets.[23]

Kryptonite's Crisis Communications Plan

Kryptonite public relations manager Donna Tocci reports that the company did all it could, as a small manufacturing company with only 25 employees, to respond effectively to the crisis. Though a business unit of Ingersoll Rand, Kryptonite handled the crisis on its own.[24]

Two days after the original post on bikeforums.net, the company issued a formal statement, informing the mainstream media that it was looking into the problem. On day three, Kryptonite began posting press releases on its website. Within a week of the original post, Kryptonite had developed its preliminary lock-exchange plan, which it finalized and announced via press release three working days later.

Kryptonite assigned all of its 25 employees a role in the crisis communications program. The company handled more than 100 media requests in the first two weeks of the crisis. In addition, Kryptonite responded to every customer who called or e-mailed in the first few days. Many of those customers instantly posted recaps of their conversations with Kryptonite on bikeforum.net. As a result, all the latest information about lock vulnerabilities and the Kryptonite lock-exchange program were instantly available online. Unfortunately, the information was neither posted by nor controlled by Krypotonite—a big mistake in the age of the blogosphere.

As a manufacturer, Tocci notes, Kryptonite faced challenges that might not affect other types of businesses. On the Friday before the original post, the company received an after-hours, anonymous voice-mail message from a caller claiming to have the ability to pop a Kryptonite lock with a Bic pen. What was the company to do? Stop production, alert distributors, issue a warning to consumers—on the basis of an anonymous phone call? What would your organization do under similar circumstances?

As a manufacturer, the company had to iron out issues related to the design and production of new cylinders—as well as fulfillment, shipping, customs, and other challenges—before it could spring into action. At the end of the day, Kryptonite reengineered its line in 9 months and exchanged over 380,000 locks in 10 months. Suppose Kryptonite, in panic, had jumped the gun and announced its lock-exchange plan before getting its manufacturing ducks in a row, and had failed to deliver as promised? The company's public relations crisis would have escalated.

Kryptonite's Exchange Program Wins Over Customers, If Not Bloggers

It's important to note that Kryptonite does not sell directly to the end user, the biker. Kryptonite sells to distributors, who in turn sell to dealers, who sell locks to individual consumers. Kryptonite's primary communications channel is, therefore, the distributor.

Two weeks after the blog mob attacked, Kryptonite attended the Interbike trade show in Las Vegas. Attended by some 20,000 dealers and distributors, the trade show gave Kryptonite the opportunity to meet one-on-one with distributors and dealers, explain the lock-exchange program, and start to rebuild trust.

Kryptonite instituted a turnkey lock-exchange program, taking care of consumers first and then replacing the inventories of distributors and dealers. All tubular-cylinder-lock owners had to do was visit www.kryptonite.com and register. When reengineered locks became available, lock owners sent in their old locks and received new ones, postage paid.

In spite of bloggers' claims that the company didn't communicate, Kryptonite claims to have received hundreds of letters from customers commending the company on its lock-exchange program and customer service. These are, Kryptonite believes, customers for life.

Moving forward, Kryptonite reports that it is well on its way to regaining shelf space from competitors who had temporarily usurped their position. Preliminary results from a 2005 brand study show that, a year after the blog attack, most consumers either never heard the story or felt it didn't affect them. Kryptonite remains the number-one bicycle lock company.[25]

How Would Kryptonite Handle a Blog Bashing Next Time?

Kryptonite's virulent blog bashing serves as a cautionary tale to all organizations, regardless of industry, size, or status as a private or public entity. The blogosphere has changed the rules of engagement when it comes to communicating with the media and other important audiences. What started as a legitimate post on bikeforums.net spread with the type of lightning speed and fierce passion that has never been seen outside the blogosphere. Bloggers who are passionate about biking (commuters, messengers, college students) felt betrayed by Kryptonite's failure to communicate to the blogosphere. That feeling of betrayal—which was not felt by distributors, dealers, and consumers who don't rely on the blogosphere for information—permeated the blogosphere throughout the Kryptonite ordeal.[26]

In the age of blogs, a company in crisis will be pushed for answers immediately from passionate and influential people who, through their blogs, have the means to help sell or sink your side of the story, as well as your organization's reputation.

Having learned this lesson the hard way, Kryptonite's Tocci says the company would never again bypass the blogosphere in favor of the mainstream media. Postcrisis, Kryptonite has now undertaken a program of building relationships with key bloggers—an essential activity that all organizations are advised to undertake now, in advance of a potential disaster, not attempt in midcrisis.

In addition, Kryptonite would act sooner to communicate with online audiences via external forums and its own corporate website. In retrospect, Tocci says, Kryptonite would have benefited by announcing, "We're working on a lock-exchange program" on its corporate website and bike forums a day or two after the attack began. Should Kryptonite face another crisis down the road, the company will take advantage of bikeforums.net and other message boards to tell its side of the story early in the process.[27]

For a review of best practices designed to help keep blogstorms at bay, see Chapter 22.

Recap and Blog Action Plan

1. *Forbes* calls blogs the "the ultimate vehicle for brand-bashing, personal attacks, political extremism, and smear campaigns."[28] Be proactive. Prepare today for the blog attack that is likely to hit tomorrow.

2. Fully 65 percent of bloggers say e-mail is the best way for an organization to make contact and report an erroneous post.[29] To minimize damage and reduce the number of links to an erroneous post, be sure to contact the blogger as soon as you become aware of an error.

3. Blogs operate in real time, and bloggers want their information right now. Business can no longer afford to communicate messages to and through the traditional mainstream media alone.

CHAPTER 22

BEST PRACTICES HELP KEEP BLOGSTORMS AT BAY

Death by blog is not really the way to go.
—NEIL FRENCH, FORMER CREATIVE DIRECTOR, WPP GROUP, QUOTED IN *TIME*[1]

When it comes to the blogosphere, the best offense is definitely a good defense. To that end, organizations that are eager to avert a disastrous blog attack (or recover as fully and quickly as possible from a blogstorm that simply can't be stopped) are advised to institute best-practices guidelines for handling attacks. This chapter lays out a suggested procedure.

Monitor the Blogosphere

A blog search found 675,000 entries by employees, franchisees, and customers talking about McDonald's in one 90-day period.[2] If you want to know what bloggers are saying about your organization, subscribe to blog search engines such as Google News Alerts (www.google.com/alerts), Pub-Sub (www.pubsub.com), DayPop (www.daypop.com), Technorati (www.technorati.com), Feedster (www.feedster.com), IceRocket (www.icerocket.com), or BlogPulse (www.blogpulse.com) to find out just what bloggers have to say—about your organization, executives, products, blogs, competitors, and just about any topic you can think of. The phrase "knowledge is power" was never as true as it is in the blogosphere.

Acknowledge the Power of the Blogosphere

Bloggers complain that most companies don't realize how influential blogs are.[3] That's not surprising, considering that 62 percent of Internet users don't even know what the term *blog* means.[4] Your organization's early acknowledgment of influential bloggers who are covering your company and industry will help establish your presence as a company that "gets" the power of the blog and will help create top-of-mind awareness for your business, its people, and products.

Be Proactive

As the Kryptonite disaster illustrates, you cannot wait until tomorrow to start building important relationships with influencers—including customer evangelists, brand bloggers, and your organization's biggest critics—in the blogosphere. You must act right now, before disaster strikes. Midcrisis, when you are juggling media calls and responding to customer fears, is no time to launch your blog networking program.

Put Your Own Employee-Bloggers to Work

Your organization's official, corporate business blog, the blogs operated by employees on company time, and the personal blogs that are published by employees at home after working hours can be effective tools in the battle to position your company, persuade readers of the validity of your message, and counter damaging lies, rumors, or disparaging remarks other bloggers may make about your company.

Establish Relationships with Influential Bloggers

The blogosphere is a community. When you start your business blog, be sure to e-mail the most influential bloggers in your industry to let them know what your blog is all about. If you want to make a good impression, send personalized e-mail messages, rather than form e-mail or an introductory press release. Although most bloggers say they prefer to be contacted via e-mail, merely 16 percent of bloggers surveyed report receiving personalized e-mail from company executives or PR reps interested in establishing a relationship.[5] For even greater impact, consider sending influential bloggers product samples for their use and review on their blogs.

Nurture and Grow Blogger Relationships

Sending out a personalized introductory e-mail is the beginning, not the end, of relationship building in the blogosphere. More than half (56 percent) of bloggers report that they "don't know" what company representative they interact with most often.[6] A personal, first-name-basis relationship will reap enormous dividends should you ever need to call on bloggers to aid your company in a crisis situation. Note: 35 percent of bloggers say they'd rather interact with a company employee who blogs, than product/brand managers (26 percent), midlevel employees (21 percent), or company executives (19 percent).[7] Put that knowledge to work by engaging employee-bloggers as the company's liaisons with the blogosphere.

Recruit Customer Evangelists

When looking for product information, fully 63 percent of bloggers say they trust other bloggers most, versus 6 percent who most trust corporate blogs.[8] That said, get to work locating and nurturing your organization's *superfans,* the customer evangelists who would be happy to write about your products and services on their sites.

Engage Brand Bloggers

Beyond customer evangelists, brand bloggers are the fanatics who are devoted to writing about their favorite brands on their own dedicated blogs, at their own expense, on their own time. Brand bloggers devote themselves to writing—mainly positively, but occasionally negatively—about the brands they feel passionately about.

Monitor the blogosphere to determine if there are any brand bloggers out there writing about your company. If you locate one, congratulations! Now get to work establishing and growing a relationship with that brand blogger. Your goal is not to turn the brand blogger into a PR tool. Your goal is to engage the brand blogger one on one, and in the process make a valuable communications channel available to the organization, should you ever need to communicate a message quickly and via a reliable source.

Be Transparent and Trustworthy

As part of the organization's blog rules, be sure to outlaw blatant cheerleading for the company or its products—that approach will earn you the disdain of bloggers. Candid, unscripted commentary from employee-bloggers—a mixture of positive and negative business-related content plus personal commentary—will go a long way toward building trust among bloggers.

File a "Cybersmear" Lawsuit

A growing number of companies are suing bloggers and other Internet users who post (often anonymously) critical, negative, embarrassing, or attack content. To that end, companies increasingly are asking the courts to force Internet service providers to reveal the identities of anonymous bloggers who post defamatory statements. The courts, however, have not been consistent in their rulings. Until the courts work this issue out, be aware that the backlash (in the blogosphere and the mainstream media) against companies that sue individual bloggers sometimes can be worse than the original blog attack. Consult with legal counsel and be sure to weigh the risks and costs against the potential benefits before you sue.

Recap and Blog Action Plan

1. Institute the blog best practices and rules detailed in this book to help minimize the risk of a costly and protracted workplace blog disaster.

PART 8

PUTTING BUSINESS BLOGS TO WORK

IBM and Edelman Share Blog Secrets, Strategies, and Success Stories

CHAPTER 23

Q & A WITH IBM

Blog Central Keeps IBM Employees at the Forefront of Technology

IBM, a publicly traded $96 billion corporation with 329,000 employees worldwide, is a leader in the "invention, development, and manufacture of the industry's most advanced information technologies, including computer systems, software, storage systems, and microelectronics."[1] With its roots in information technology, IBM physically enables technology and helps simplify and enrich the experience. Through its own internal blog program, IBM is exploring the potential of business blogging, just as the company once helped pioneer and engineer the web for business advantage.

At the heart of IBM's blog program is *Blog Central*. Through intranet-based Blog Central, some 2,500 IBMers are test-driving their own internal blogs and communicating with one another inside IBM. Topics range from the deeply technical, to requests for help on business questions, to personal diary-type reflections. In addition, about 1,800 IBMers have registered with Blog Central in order to read and respond to their colleagues' blogs.[2]

Before launching its internal blog program, IBM first drafted an employee blogging policy, which the company has been kind enough to share with readers of *Blog Rules* (see Chapter 24).

The author's Q&A session with IBM's Corporate Affairs Director Brian Doyle is excerpted as follows.[3]

Q. What is the genesis of IBM's corporate blog program?

A. At IBM, we've actively embraced new media and encourage our employees to explore and learn from new technologies like blogs and podcasts. We have 329,000 employees worldwide, all of whom are smart, inquisitive people with information to share. As new technology tools become available to help further the exchange of information among employees internally and with our customers and other third parties externally, IBM actively works to give employees access to them. Our employees' use of new technology tools gives IBM a chance to assess their potential as enablers of communication and to determine how the technology might best be put to work for our customers.

IBM has always encouraged employees to be early adopters of new technologies. During the early days of the Internet, we encouraged employees to go online and explore the web. Rather than being concerned about productivity, we view employees' exploration of new technologies as a way for the individual and the corporation to gain understanding and develop expertise. The same now holds true for blogs.

With its roots in information technology, blogging is in line with the type of open standards IBM has always championed. IBM physically enables technology and helps simplify and enrich the experience. IBM helped pioneer and engineer the web for business advantage. Now we are doing the same with blogs.

IBM is not a consumer products company. We help large enterprises serve their customers. By actively encouraging employees to blog, and to learn all they can about the technology and its business communications power, we gain insights that we can put to work for the benefit of our customers and the consumers they serve.

Q. What is the goal of IBM's blog program?

A. When Louis Gerstner Jr. became chairman and CEO of IBM in 1993, he refocused the company on the customer and our relationships and communications with the customer. No longer the proverbial 800-pound gorilla that produced machines and let customers figure out how to use them, IBM became a company that is focused on creating solutions and delivering services to customers. Our current chairman, Samuel Palmisano, has sharpened and accelerated that focus. Blogs, as well as podcasts, are new media that fit perfectly into IBM's solutions-oriented approach.

Blogging is a good way to build relationships, demonstrate thought leadership, and help people develop an affinity for IBM. Blogs are such open and freewheeling new media that you might not think of them as corporate tools. On the contrary, blogs are all about collaboration and innovation. As our employees have pursued the capabilities of blogs, we have found them to be very good social networking and relationship-building tools.

Q. How does the IBM podcast program fit into the company's new media strategy?

A. In mid-2005, we introduced both blogs and podcasts, with accompanying written policies. (A podcast is an audio version of a blog, broadcast over the Internet.) We currently produce external podcasts for the investment community and other outside audiences, as well as internal podcasts for employees.

Podcasting, like blogging, is an effective way to position IBM as both a company of experts and the customer's partner. Through IBM podcasts, audiences have the opportunity to explore advances in technology and take a look at what the future holds for cities, banking, shopping, the home, and all aspects of business and life. By opening and engaging in dialogue that is of interest to podcast audiences, IBM is viewed as a leader by customers, the public, the investment community, and our employees.

Q. How are your podcasts doing?

A. Monitoring has revealed just how popular IBM's podcasts are. At times, we have ranked in the top 10 out of thousands of listings on iTunes.

Q. How did IBM introduce blogging to employees?

A. To begin with, we thoroughly considered the implications of allowing employees to blog and podcast. We considered the potential release of confidential information, among other risks. In the end, we determined that the shared values of trust and personal responsibility are IBM's foundations. Plus, we view the blog as just one more communications tool. If someone really wants to reveal confidential information, that person can easily do it by phone, fax, or e-mail.

Because we are determined to make new technologies as appealing and accessible as possible for employees, we developed quick-start blogging and podcasting tools, including templates and tutorials, which are available online via the employee intranet. We also spotlight selected "best of" examples of employee and third-party blogs and podcasts to help employees design and develop their own tools.

At the heart of IBM's blog program is what we call "Blog Central." Through intranet-based Blog Central, some 2,500 IBMers are test driving their own internal blogs and communicating with one another inside IBM. Topics range from the deeply technical, to requests for help on business unit questions, to personal diary-type reflections.

In addition to those 2,500 bloggers, about 1,800 IBMers have registered with Blog Central in order to read and respond to their colleagues' blogs.

Blog Central provides employees with a learning curve environment. In six months, the blogs that are currently active probably will have morphed into something different. Are there likely to be some missteps? Sure, but we believe the risks are worth it.

What does the future hold? We are actively pursuing a plan to link IBM employee-bloggers to the outside world. But for now, Blog Central strictly supports internal blogging.

Q. In addition to the 2,500 employees who are blogging internally on Blog Central, does IBM operate any external blogs?

A. We have several external, or customer-facing blogs on which we encourage intelligent dialogue and information exchange. Because IBM makes the chips for leading video gaming systems, IBM's systems group operates a gaming blog, http://www.gametomorrow.com/blog, designed to engage the video gaming community.

In addition, IBM's health care group operates an external blog to discuss the ways in which IT has changed health care delivery systems. That blog, http://healthnex.typepad.com, which also hosts discussions about topics like genetic privacy, is doing a good job of attracting comments from leaders in the field of health care.

Q. How did IBM develop its blogging policy and guidelines?

A. Clearly blog guidelines were needed before the program could get underway. We enlisted a group of IBM employees, who happened to be blogging on their own time, to draft the company's guidelines. The IBM Blogging Policy and Guidelines were published in May 2005 (see Chapter 24).

The policy makes it clear that employees must abide by IBM's business conduct guidelines when blogging. Employee-bloggers must behave in an ethical manner, protect the company's confidential data, and adhere to the policies that steer IBM's business. We also encourage employees to publish a disclaimer stating their blog posts reflect their own views, not IBM's.

IBM makes no distinction between personal blogging at home and business-related blogging at the office. Whether an employee is standing on a soap box in Central Park or sitting in the office blogging, a violation is a violation.

Annually, employees are required to sign a form acknowledging that they have read and will abide by IBM's business conduct policy.

Q. How is IBM's blogging policy distributed to employees?

A. On the employee intranet, which is the central repository of information for our employees worldwide.

Q. Does the legal department review employees' copy pre-post?

A. The blogger-in-chief is responsible for managing IBM's blog space. Copy is not reviewed in advance of posting. However, if posts or comments run counter to the guidelines or are otherwise offensive, the blogger in-chief will jump in, either publicly in a blog format or individually, to correct the problem.

Q. Are third-party comments screened before they are posted on IBM's two external blogs?

A. No.

Q. How does blogging benefit IBM?

A. Internal blogging gives employees a powerful new way to collaborate and innovate. External blogging and podcasting enable IBM employees to engage in an organic, intellectual interchange with outside experts and industry leaders. They demonstrate to clients, the investment community, policy makers, and other target audiences just how smart and innovative IBM's employees are.

Q. How will blogs affect traditional public relations and media relations?

A. Blogs move the corporation toward greater interaction with unconventional advocates and influencers. Business is no longer reliant solely on mainstream journalists to communicate messages. Other audiences and influencers now have a bearing on an organization's success, image, and brand equity. In the age of blogs, we no longer measure press clips by the pound to determine public relations success.

Q. Any advice for other companies that may be considering starting an employee-blogging program?

A. The new era of interpersonal communications between big enterprises comes down to the level of the individual. For global enterprises, that concept demands a rethinking of what it means to release information solely through "official" channels. Business must think about new technology tools, including blogs and podcasts, that have the power to transform the way people interact.

When it comes to blogging and podcasting, the train has left the station. It behooves organizations of all types to recognize the growth and popularity of blogs. Give serious thought to engaging with the blogosphere. Act now to evaluate and determine how your organization is going to manage blogs, and perhaps podcasts, to the organization's advantage.

The choice is simple: Be paralyzed with fear over the concept of open communications channels, or put a blog policy in place and start using these new media in a strategic way.

CHAPTER 24

IBM BLOGGING POLICY AND GUIDELINES

Introduction: Responsible Engagement in Innovation and Dialogue

Whether or not an IBMer chooses to create or participate in a blog or a wiki or other form of online publishing or discussion is his or her own decision. However, it is very much in IBM's interest—and, we believe, in each IBMer's own—to be aware of this sphere of information, interaction, and idea exchange:

To learn: As an innovation-based company, we believe in the importance of open exchange and learning—between IBM and its clients, and among the many constituents of our emerging business and societal ecosystem. The rapidly growing phenomenon of blogging and online dialogue are emerging as important arenas for that kind of engagement and learning.

To contribute: IBM—as a business, as an innovator, and as a corporate citizen—makes important contributions to the world, to the future of business and technology, and to public dialogue on a broad range of societal issues. As our business activities increasingly focus on the provision of transformational insight and high-value innovation—whether to business clients or those in the public, educational, or health sectors—it becomes increasingly important for IBM and IBMers to share with the world the exciting things we're learning and doing, and to learn from others.

In 1997, IBM recommended that its employees get out onto the Net—at a time when many companies were seeking to restrict their employees' Internet access. We continue to advocate IBMers' responsible involvement today in this new, rapidly growing space of relationship, learning, and collaboration.

Guidelines for IBM Bloggers: Executive Summary

1. Know and follow IBM's Business Conduct Guidelines.
2. Blogs, wikis, and other forms of online discourse are individual interactions, not corporate communications. IBMers are personally responsible for their posts. Be mindful that what you write will be public for a long time—protect your privacy.
3. Identify yourself—name and, when relevant, role at IBM—when you blog about IBM or IBM-related matters. And write in the first person. You must make it clear that you are speaking for yourself and not on behalf of IBM.
4. If you publish a blog or post to a blog outside of IBM and it has something to do with work you do or subjects associated with IBM, use a disclaimer such as this: "The postings on this site are my own and don't necessarily represent IBM's positions, strategies, or opinions."
5. Respect copyright, fair use, and financial disclosure laws.
6. Don't provide IBM's or another's confidential or other proprietary information. Ask permission to publish or report on conversations that are meant to be private or internal to IBM.
7. Don't cite or reference clients, partners, or suppliers without their approval.
8. Respect your audience. Don't use ethnic slurs, personal insults, obscenity, etc., and show proper consideration for others' privacy and for topics that may be considered objectionable or inflammatory—such as politics and religion.
9. Find out who else is blogging on the topic, and cite them.
10. Don't pick fights, be the first to correct your own mistakes, and don't alter previous posts without indicating that you have done so.
11. Try to add value. Provide worthwhile information and perspective.

Guidelines for IBM Bloggers: Detailed Discussion

1. The IBM Business Conduct Guidelines (BCGs) and laws provide the foundation for IBM's policies and guidelines on weblogs (blogs).

The same principles and guidelines that apply to IBMers' activities in general, as codified in the IBM Business Conduct Guidelines, apply to IBMers' activities online. This includes forms of online publishing and discussion, such as weblogs (blogs) and wikis.

As outlined in the Business Conduct Guidelines, IBM fully respects the legal rights of our employees in all countries in which we operate. In general, what you do on your own time is your affair. However, activities in or outside of work that affect your IBM job performance, the performance of others, or IBM's business interests are a proper focus for company policy.

2. IBM supports open dialogue and the exchange of ideas.

IBM regards blogs as primarily a form of communication and relationship among individuals. When the company wishes to communicate publicly as a company—whether to the marketplace or to the general public—it has well established means to do so. Only those officially designated by IBM have the authorization to speak on behalf of the company.

However, IBM believes in dialogue among IBMers and with our partners, clients, members of the many communities in which we participate, and the general public. Such dialogue is inherent in our business model of innovation, and in our commitment to the development of open standards. We believe that IBMers can both derive and provide important benefits from exchanges of perspective.

One of IBMers' core values is "trust and personal responsibility in all relationships." As a company, IBM trusts—and expects—IBMers to exercise personal responsibility whenever they blog. This includes not violating the trust of those with whom they are engaging. IBMers should not use this medium for covert marketing or public relations. If and when members of IBM's Communications, Marketing, Sales, or other functions engaged in advocacy for the company have the authorization to participate in blogs, they should identify themselves as such.

2a. What does an IBMer's personal responsibility mean when blogging?

A blog is a tool individuals can use to share their insights, express their opinions, and communicate within the context of a globally distributed conversation. As with all tools, it has proper and improper uses. While IBM encourages all of its employees to join a global conversation, it is important for IBMers who choose to do so to understand what is recommended, expected and required when they discuss IBM-related topics, whether at work or on their own time.

2b. Know the IBM Business Conduct Guidelines (BCGs).

If you have any confusion about whether you ought to post something on your blog, chances are the BCGs will resolve it. Pay particular attention to what the BCGs have to say about proprietary information, about avoiding misrepresentation, and about competing in the field. If, after checking the BCG's, you are still unclear as to the propriety of a post, it is best to refrain and seek the advice of management.

3a. Be who you are.

Some bloggers work anonymously, using pseudonyms or false screen names. IBM discourages that in blogs, wikis, or other forms of online participation that relate to IBM, our business, or issues with which the company is engaged. We believe in transparency and honesty. If you are blogging about your work for IBM, we encourage you to use your real name, be clear who you are, and identify that you work for IBM. Nothing gains you notice in the "blogosphere" more than honesty—or dishonesty. If you have a vested interest in something you are discussing, be the first to point it out. But also be smart about protecting yourself and your privacy. What you publish will be around for a long time, so consider the content carefully and also be judicious in disclosing personal details.

3b. Speak in the first person.

Use your own voice; bring your own personality to the forefront; say what is on your mind.

4a. Use a disclaimer.

Whether you publish a blog or participate in someone else's, make it clear that what you say there is representative of your views and opinions and not necessarily the views and opinions of IBM. At a minimum in your own blog, you should include the following standard legal disclaimer language: "The postings on this site are my own and don't necessarily represent IBM's positions, strategies, or opinions."

4b. Managers and executives: Take note.

This standard disclaimer does not by itself exempt IBM managers and executives from a special responsibility when blogging. By virtue of their position, they must consider whether personal thoughts they publish may be misunderstood as expressing IBM positions. And a manager should assume that his or her team will read what is written. A blog is not the place to communicate IBM policies to IBM employees.

5. Respect copyright and fair use laws.

For IBM's protection and well as your own, it is critical that you show proper respect for the laws governing copyright and fair use of copyrighted material owned by others, including IBM's own copyrights and brands. You should never quote more than short excerpts of someone else's work. And it is good general blogging practice to link to others' work. Keep in mind that laws will be different depending on where you live and work.

6a. Protect confidential and proprietary information.

You must make sure you do not disclose or use IBM confidential or proprietary information or that of any other person or company on any blog. For example, ask permission to publish someone's picture or a conversation that was meant to be private.

6b. IBM's business performance.

You must not comment on confidential IBM financial information such as IBM's future business performance, business plans, or prospects anywhere in world. This includes statements about an upcoming quarter or future periods, or information about alliances, and applies to anyone including conversations with Wall Street analysts, press, or other third parties (including friends). IBM policy is not to comment on rumors in any way. Do not deny or affirm them—or suggest either denial or affirmation in subtle ways.

7. Protect IBM's clients, business partners and suppliers.

Clients, partners, or suppliers should not be cited or obviously referenced without their approval. On your blog, never identify a client, partner, or supplier by name without permission and never discuss confidential details of a client engagement. It is acceptable to discuss general details about kinds of projects and to use non-identifying pseudonyms for a client (e.g., Client 123) so long as the information provided does not violate any nondisclosure agreements that may be in place with the client or make it easy for someone to identify the client. Furthermore, your blog is not the place to conduct business with a client.

8. Respect your audience and your coworkers.

Remember that IBM is a global organization whose employees and clients reflect a diverse set of customs, values, and points of view. Don't be afraid to be yourself, but do so respectfully. This includes not only the obvious (no ethnic slurs, personal insults, obscenity, etc.) but also proper consideration of privacy and of topics that may be considered objectionable or inflammatory—such as politics and religion. If your blog is hosted on an IBM-owned property, avoid these topics and focus on subjects that are business-related.

If your blog is self-hosted, use your best judgment and be sure to make it clear that the views and opinions expressed are yours alone and do not represent the official views of IBM. Further, blogs hosted outside of IBM's protected intranet environment must never be used for internal communications among fellow employees. It is fine for IBMers to disagree, but please don't use your external blog to air your differences in an inappropriate manner.

Add value.

Blogs that are hosted on IBM-owned domains should be used in a way that adds value to IBM's business. If it helps you, your coworkers, our clients, or our partners to do their jobs and solve problems; if it helps to improve knowledge or skills; if it contributes directly or indirectly to the improvement of IBM's products, processes, and policies; or if it helps to promote IBM's values, then it is adding value. Though not directly business-related, background information you choose to share about yourself, such as information about your family or personal interests, may be useful in helping establish a relationship between you and your readers, but it is entirely your choice whether to share this information.

Apply the skills and values learned from participation in IBM jams, IBM forums, and other kinds of online collaboration.

Although a relatively small percentage of the IBM population has thus far participated actively in blogs, we have a deep well of experience in online collaboration—perhaps deeper than any other company in the world. Starting with the VM Fora in the 1980s, and extending up to our emeetings, teamrooms, and companywide jams on w3 today, IBMers have honed skills, wisdom, and creativity in many forms of online collaboration and engagement. We should bring this experience to bear in blogs and wikis.

For instance, think about constructive forms of facilitation you've seen in jams or the IBM forums. What did those IBMers do that helped develop the discussion, moved it forward, brought people together who were making complementary points, encouraged others to express themselves—or to push themselves? Blogs aren't restricted to expressing opinions, or disputing opinions, or discussing products or services or one's personal life. They can also be a forum for genuine public discussion and learning—and IBMers can play a fruitful, mature, and constructive role in helping that happen.

9. Know your fellow bloggers.

The most successful bloggers are those who pay attention to what others are saying about the topic they want to write about, and generously reference and link to them. Who's blogging on the topics that most interest you? On the Internet, a quick way to find out who's saying what is to use the search tools on Technorati, DayPop, or Blogdigger. Drop your fellow bloggers a note to introduce yourself and your blog. There is also an informal community of IBM bloggers, so you can quickly find out which of your peers are part of the conversation.

10. Don't pick fights.

When you see misrepresentations made about IBM in the media, by analysts, or by other bloggers, you may certainly use your blog—or join someone else's—to point that out. Always do so with respect and with the facts. Also, if you speak about a competitor, you must make sure that what you say is factual and that it does not disparage the competitor. You should avoid arguments. Brawls may earn traffic, but nobody wins in the end. Don't try to settle scores or goad competitors or others into inflammatory debates. Here and in other areas of public discussion, make sure that what you are saying is factually correct.

Be the first to respond to your own mistakes.

If you make an error, be up front about your mistake and correct it quickly. If you choose to modify an earlier post, make it clear that you have done so.

Use your best judgment.

Remember that there are always consequences to what you write. If you're about to post something that makes you even the slightest bit uncomfortable, review the suggestions above and think about why that is. If you're still unsure, and the post is about IBM business, feel free to discuss your proposed post with your manager. Ultimately, however, you have sole responsibility for what you choose to post to your blog.

Don't forget your day job.

You should make sure that blogging does not interfere with your job or commitments to customers.

IBM Corporation. Published May 16, 2005

CHAPTER 25

Q & A WITH EDELMAN

We service clients, not Wall Street.

POSTED ON THE WELCOME PAGE, WWW.EDELMAN.COM[1]

Communications giant Edelman is the only remaining major independent public relations firm operating today. With 1,900 employees in 43 offices, Edelman currently has two executives operating facing-out business blogs— CEO Richard Edelman and director of the firm's employee engagement practice Christopher Hannegan. In addition, Edelman works with clients on the development of their internal and external blogs.

Through the publication of white papers such as "Talking from the Inside Out: The Rise of Employee Bloggers,"[2] and "New Frontiers in Employee Communications"[3]; and surveys including "Engaging the Blogosphere: An Edelman/Technorati Study,"[4] and "The Sixth Annual Edelman Trust Barometer: A Global Study of Opinion Leaders,"[5] Edelman has assumed a position of corporate thought leadership within the blogosphere.

Before launching its corporate blog program, Edelman first started with policy, which the company has been kind enough to share with readers of *Blog Rules* (see Chapter 26).

The author's Q & A session with Edelman's Christopher Hannegan, senior vice president and employee engagement practice director, is excerpted as follows.[6]

Q. How is business blogging changing the ways in which companies communicate? What impact is blogging having on traditional business communications channels, public relations, and advertising?

A. Blogs enable companies to build the type of grassroots relationships with customers that simply didn't exist before. Business blogs also facilitate relationships with influential bloggers who may be writing about the company.

When it comes to managing corporate reputations, blogs are changing the role individual employees have traditionally played—making that role more dynamic. Because employee-bloggers are viewed as "just ordinary guys," there is a higher built-in level of trust among other bloggers and readers in general. At the end of the day, greater trust leads to stronger relationships.

It is extremely important to establish and grow relationships with influencers in the blogosphere. Do your homework. Who is talking about issues that are important to your company? Who shares your company's viewpoint? Which bloggers promote an opposing point of view?

Once you have identified key bloggers, start interacting with them in a constructive way. The goal is to build relationships with influential bloggers who can help protect your corporate reputation should you someday get into trouble.

Q. How is blogging affecting media relations? How do organizations keep their employee-bloggers from talking directly to the media?

A. It is impossible to prevent all employees from talking to the media. And you don't necessarily want to stop employees from talking to the media, either. As a company representative, the average employee's credibility tops the CEO by a three-to-one margin, according to our 2005 trust study. You want to put that credibility to good use. Just be sure to put written policies in place to ensure that the interaction between employees and the media is a positive experience for the organization and the individuals involved.

Remember, also, that if your policy on talking to the media is too restrictive, if management tries to keep too close a lid on company news, then some employees may rebel and post more information than management would like on their blogs.

Q. Where do you stand on pre-post editing? Should employers assign someone from the legal or public relations department to review all blog posts and comments prior to publication?

A. As long as clear disclaimers exist to notify readers that the comments made reflect the opinions of the individual blogger, not the organization, then posts should be made freely and without editing. The tendency of PR people and lawyers is just too great to edit copy and censor content. Once you start that, you might as well stop blogging. Blogging derives its credibility from its honesty and transparency. That said, it certainly is acceptable for organizations to monitor blog content for obscenity and other offensive language that violates company policy. At Edelman, for example, all incoming posts and comments go through a screening process for obscenity.

Q. What about public companies? Shouldn't public companies be particularly concerned about having all blog entries reviewed pre-post by the investor relations department or legal counsel?

A. This is where written guidelines come into play. Formal guidelines provide mutually agreed-upon criteria under which employees operate and employers control business risks. Blogging is no different from any other business communications tool. Electronic communications is not a new idea to companies. Just as company guidelines would prevent an employee from leaking insider information to the *Wall Street Journal* in violation of SEC rules, so, too, should guidelines be in place to help manage the blog activity of employees—public or private.

Q. As an electronic business communications tool, what benefits do blogs offer?

A. Relationship building is the number-one reason to blog. Business blogs play a tremendous role in building and maintaining customer relationships, while enhancing corporate reputations. Blogs also can be more effective than advertising at creating buzz and conversation. That said, companies might be better off redeploying their advertising dollars and resources for grass-roots blogs.

In addition, blogs provide organizations with a channel to conduct conversations with constituencies that might not be reached otherwise. Blogs give organizations the power to organize and share information and experiences among employees. IBM is the poster child for successful internal blogging. Traditional knowledge management has been left in the dust by internal blogs, which make information readily available to the employees who need it, when they need it.

Finally, a business blog can help propel a company to the forefront of its industry, making it the company of the moment. Thanks to the blog, a company may suddenly find itself a hip brand, which can be a big boost to recruiting and employee morale.

Q. From the perspective of a professional communicator, what are the downsides to business blogging?

A. Companies can be paralyzed by what they perceive as a loss of control when employees blog. Blogging does, after all, provide employees with a channel to express individual perspectives to external readers.

Some employees will use the blog as a way to vent about their employers. That risk is greatest in organizations that have not done a good job of engaging employees. If employees have no other way to express themselves or vent their frustrations with management, then they are more likely to use the blog to do so.

On the other hand, organizations that do provide employees with other avenues to work through frustrations find that the tone of employee blogs is overwhelmingly positive by a four-to-one margin.

Finally, perhaps the greatest blog-related risk employers face is the negative publicity, in the mainstream media and blogosphere, that can result from firing employee-bloggers. Put written blog guidelines in place to reduce the likelihood that employee-bloggers will act in a manner that warrants their termination for blogging.

Q. What should a company do if it finds itself under assault in the blogosphere?

A. This is why it is so important to establish and nurture relationships with your employee-bloggers, as well as the influential bloggers who cover your company and industry. If you find yourself under assault, about the only thing you can do is quickly marshal the forces of your current employee-bloggers. (This will be a problem for many companies, since they have not yet identified their own employee-bloggers.) Recruit your employee-bloggers to help manage the situation in the blogosphere. Short of that, launch an immediate company blog program utilizing the services of a handful of lower-level employees who can act as experts in whatever area is plaguing the company at the moment.

Whichever approach you take, be transparent. Bloggers can smell a rat. Instruct your employee-bloggers to be forthcoming: "My company has come under assault, and as a member of the team, I want to share the facts . . ."

Q. Let's talk about CEO blogs. What does it take to make a CEO blog successful?

A. First, is the CEO really committed to blogging? The CEO's blog, just like the company blog, needs to be approached as a long-term effort. The CEO must commit to a whole new set of communications behaviors, including transparency. Many CEOs are "handled" by PR people. They are conditioned to watch what they say and be careful of how they say it. That is the exact opposite of what it takes to succeed in the blogosphere.

Time is an issue, too. The CEO, like any business blogger, needs to post regularly. If you don't have time to post at least twice a week, don't bother to blog. I don't advocate the use of a ghostwriter, but it certainly is okay to assign a staff member to help out with research and other behind-the-scenes work related to the CEO's blog. The actual writing needs to be completed by the CEO, in the CEO's voice, expressing the CEO's thoughts and opinions.

Q. Tell me about the blog that your CEO, Richard Edelman, operates.

A. Richard Edelman launched his blog in September 2004, after he felt it was vital he experience the blogosphere firsthand. He views it as a truly revolutionary channel providing voice to the general public, who then influence their peers and mainstream media, thereby turning the traditional top-down model of communications on its head. He sees that the blogosphere provides corporations (and executives) with unfiltered access to engage and listen to audiences, whether employees or avid consumers, about their company or important issues. It's a way to involve stakeholders with a very direct, timely, and conversational medium. As the CEO of the world's largest independent public relations firm, Richard views his blog as a way to discuss issues affecting his profession. As an intellectually curious guy, Richard opted to assume a gutsy position, addressing the industry's most controversial issues. Today, Richard Edelman's blog, www.edelman.com/speak_up/blog, generates 2,500 unique hits a week and provides stakeholders with a unique insight into the perspective of the CEO of one of the world's largest PR firms. In addition, Richard benefits from the insights afforded by readers and fellow bloggers.

Q. Does Edelman monitor employees' blogs?

A. We don't monitor our own employees, but we have a blog analytic partner, Intelliseek, which is now part of BuzzMetrics and helps us monitor blogs in general.

Q. Does Edelman have a blog policy? How are employees informed of the policy?

A. Blog rules are covered as part of the Edelman Principles & Code of Conduct (see Chapter 26). During orientation, all new employees receive a copy, which is incorporated into the employee handbook. In addition, all employees are required to sign an acknowledgment form, certifying that they understand the firm's rules and policies, and agree to comply with them.

CHAPTER 26

EDELMAN'S PRINCIPLES AND CODE OF CONDUCT: MAINTAINING A WEBLOG

We are still in the early days of weblogs and have examined the degree to which other companies have stated positions about employees and their creation and use of weblogs. Microsoft sums up its counsel to employees by simply stating: "Be Smart." We share this perspective, but also encourage you to consider the following nine tips if you are inclined to activate a personal non–work-related blog:

a. You agree to write under your own name.

b. You agree not to attack personally fellow employees, journalists, clients, or other stakeholders with whom you interact as an employee of Edelman.

c. You agree not to disclose any sensitive, proprietary, confidential, non-public, or financial information about the firm and/or its clients.

d. You agree not to post any material that is obscene, defamatory, profane, libelous, threatening, harassing, abusive, hateful, or embarrassing to another person or any other person or entity.

e. You agree not to post any material that is copyrighted unless you (a) are the copyright owner; (b) have the express, written permission of the copyright owner to post the copyrighted material on your blog; or (c) are reasonably sure that the use of any copyrighted material conforms to the doctrine of "fair use."

f. You agree not to post any material that violates the privacy or publicity rights of another individual.

g. You agree to conform to the rules of the *Edelman's Employee Handbook,* especially as it relates to rules regarding conduct outside of your employment.

h. You agree not to post or conduct any activity that fails to conform with any and all applicable local, state, and/or federal laws, including, without limitation, 15 U.S.C. 6501 et seq. (the "Children's Online Privacy Protection Act of 1998").

i. You acknowledge that any reliance on material, content, and/or links posted by other parties will be at your own risk. You assume full legal responsibility and liability for all actions arising from your posts.

Blogging on behalf of Edelman should be treated the same as any other official communication created by Edelman and done only with the prior consent of Edelman as applicable.

A broad array of guidelines about expected professional and personal behavior as an Edelman employee can be found in the Employee Handbook, which all employees are expected to have read and indicated that they have done so by signing an accompanying form. The handbook also addresses e-mail protocols and the handling and use of computers and laptops.

Please refer to the handbook if you need guidance in areas not addressed above.[1]

Acknowledgment of Edelman's Code of Conduct

In addition to compliance with Edelman's Code of Conduct, as an employee of Edelman, I certify to understanding the following principles and responsibilities governing my professional and ethical conduct.

To the best of my knowledge and ability:

1. I will act with honesty and integrity, avoiding actual or apparent conflicts of interest in personal and professional relationships.

2. I will provide information that is accurate, complete, objective, relevant, timely, and understandable.

3. I will comply with rules and regulations of federal, state, and local governments, and other appropriate private and public regulatory agencies.

4. I will act in good faith, responsibly, and with due care, competence, and diligence, without misrepresenting facts or allowing my independent judgment to be subordinated.

5. I will respect the confidentiality of information acquired in the course of my work except when authorized or otherwise legally obligated to disclose it. Confidential information acquired in the course of my work is never used for personal advantage.
6. I will sharpen skills important and relevant to my responsibilities.
7. I will proactively promote ethical behavior and promptly report violations of the Code of Conduct.
8. I will achieve responsible use of, and control over, all assets and resources employed by or entrusted to me.
9. I acknowledge that I am responsible and accountable for adherence to Edelman's Code of Conduct.[2]

_____

(Signature)

_____

(Date)
(original to employee's file with HR; copy kept by employee)

THIRTY-SIX BLOG RULES: BEST PRACTICES TO KEEP YOU OUT OF COURT WITH YOUR CORPORATE REPUTATION INTACT

Blog Rule #1: The blog is an electronic communications powerhouse that is likely to have greater impact on business communications and corporate reputations than e-mail, instant messaging, and traditional marketing-oriented websites combined.

Blog Rule #2: Business blogs are not necessary or appropriate for every organization. Evaluate the benefits and assess the risks before leaping into the blogosphere.

Blog Rule #3: Savvy business owners and executives must learn how to strategically and successfully manage the blogosphere today—or risk potentially unpleasant and expensive consequences tomorrow.

Blog Rule #4: It's the casual, conversational, anything-goes nature of the blog that makes it both so appealing to blog writers and readers— and so potentially dangerous to business.

Blog Rule #5: An organization without an external blog program may risk losing position, market share, reputation, and sales to tech-savvy competitors who have already recognized—and tapped into— the power of the blogosphere.

Blog Rule #6: The strategic management of blogs or any other electronic business communications tool begins with the establishment of written rules and policies governing usage and content.

Blog Rule #7: A business blog opens the organization up to potential disasters, including the loss of trade secrets, confidential information, and intellectual property; negative publicity, damaged reputations, and public embarrassment; workplace lawsuits alleging copyright infringement, defamation, sexual harassment, and other claims; court sanctions, legal settlements, and regulatory fines; and lost employee productivity.

Blog Rule #8: Management, technology, and the legal system have not yet caught up with the potential benefits and risks of business blogging.

Blog Rule #9: Strategic blog management begins with the establishment of a clear objective. In other words, why does your organization want to blog?

Blog Rule #10: Don't allow IT (or legal, records management, or human resources) to dictate your business blog program. Work as a team to implement rules, policies, and procedures based on the best practices detailed in *Blog Rules*.

Blog Rule #11: Require employees to sign a confidentiality agreement to protect trade secrets and confidential data belonging to the organization, employees, customers, business partners and other third parties. Cover blog posts and comments published on the organization's business blogs, employees' personal blogs, and other external blogs, as well.

Blog Rule #12: Use discipline to maximize employee compliance with blog rules, policies, and procedures. Put blog content and usage rules in writing, and stress the fact that the organization's rules and policies apply regardless of whether employees are blogging at the office or at home on their own time and equipment. Inform employees that any violation of the organization's rules and policies may result in disciplinary action, up to and including termination.

Blog Rule #13: Treat blog posts and comments as business records that must be retained, archived, and readily available to courts or regulators in the event of a workplace lawsuit or regulatory investigation.

Blog Rule #14: Use the establishment of your blog program as an opportunity to review all electronic communications policies. Update (or create) e-mail, instant message, Internet, intranet, and blog policies based on best practices detailed in *Blog Rules*.

Blog Rule #15: Employee training is key to compliance with blog content, usage rules, and retention policy.

Blog Rule #16: Expect to see employees' blog posts and readers' comments enter the evidence pool in sexual harassment claims, discrimination cases, and hostile work environment lawsuits.

Blog Rule #17: Enhance your organization's legal position—and increase the likelihood of successfully defending a sexual harassment or hostile work environment claim someday—by establishing a comprehensive written blog policy and enforcing that policy with a consistent program of training, technology, and discipline.

Blog Rule #18: As a third-party copyright infringer (thanks to customers' blog comments) the organization could be subject to treble damages. Seek safe-harbor protection from liability through the Digital Millennium Copyright Act (DMCA).

Blog Rule #19: A strict anti-blog policy, backed by content security technology, helps publicly traded companies and regulated firms ensure employee compliance with regulators' blog-related content, usage, and retention rules.

Blog Rule #20: The blog is all about content.

Blog Rule #21: Blogging culture demands absolute honesty. The blogosphere hates a phony!

Blog Rule #22: Assign a lawyer or other responsible party to review, edit, and—as necessary—delete readers' comments pre-post. All it takes is one inappropriate comment to trigger a workplace lawsuit, regulatory investigation, or blog mob attack.

Blog Rule #23: Blogs allow smaller companies to create immediate intimate connections with consumers and build loyalty without spending millions of dollars on traditional mainstream media advertising.

Blog Rule #24: Inappropriate content is inappropriate content, whether it's transmitted via e-mail or posted (and permalinked) on a blog. The primary difference is that risky blog content has a never-ending "viral" quality. You can count on a juicy, salacious, or otherwise unprofessional and embarrassing blog post to be read, linked to, and commented upon by countless readers for years to come.

Blog Rule #25: Incorporate the rules of blog etiquette into the organization's blog policy. By addressing and enforcing blog etiquette, employers can maximize civil business behavior in the blogosphere while minimizing the likelihood of inappropriate entries that might offend readers, trigger litigation, or otherwise harm the organization.

Blog Rule #26: Use blog monitoring tools to track what is being written about your organization and help control comment spam and splog.

Blog Rule #27: Although technology struggles to solve the challenge of surging splog attacks and comment spam, business bloggers (and individuals who are blogging at home) are advised to do what they can on their own to battle spam in the blogosphere.

Blog Rule #28: Blogging can get you fired! Hundreds of employees have been fired, or dooced, for blogging about their employers.

Blog Rule #29: Blogging can get you sued! Given the growing popularity of blogs and the propensity of bloggers to use their sites to opine on people, products, service quality, and businesses, the potential for litigation (aimed at organizations and individuals) is huge.

Blog Rule #30: The First Amendment does not protect bloggers.

Blog Rule #31: Thanks to incoming links, outgoing links, permalinks, ping services, and syndication, a factually inaccurate or otherwise damaging post can bounce around the Internet from one blog to millions of other blogs forever—archived and ever-accessible to new readers.

Blog Rule #32: Blogs are rapidly—and forever—changing the way PR people and media relations professionals do business.

Blog Rule #33: It pays to put customer evangelists and brand bloggers to work creating buzz in the blogosphere.

Blog Rule #34: Blogging by CEOs and other C-level executives who want to engage internal and external stakeholders is on the rise.

Blog Rule #35: Blogging may not be the best way for CEOs to communicate confidential, potentially embarrassing, or otherwise damaging information to employees and other insiders. There simply is no taking your words back once your blog post goes live.

Blog Rule #36: Blogs are a phenomenal vehicle for attacking companies, brands, and individuals. Be proactive. Prepare today for the blog attack that is likely to hit tomorrow.

SAMPLE BLOG POLICIES

Blog Policy 1

The Company provides employees with blog access for the benefit of the organization and customers. Employees using the Company blog are responsible for maintaining the organization's public image and communicating with the blogosphere appropriately. To that end, the Company has established the following Blog Policy.

Employees are required to adhere to the Company's Blog Policy when at the office (or elsewhere) using the Company's business blog system for business or personal reasons. Employees also are expected to comply with the Company's Blog Policy when at home (or elsewhere) using a personal blog for business or personal reasons.

Violations of the Company's Blog Policy, whether they occur on the Company's blog or the employee's own personal blog, will result in disciplinary action, up to and including termination.

1. I will not use a pseudonym, fake name, or otherwise blog anonymously. I will identify myself by name as the publisher/writer of my business and personal blogs.
2. I will identify myself as an employee of the Company, including my title, in all business-related blog posts published on the Company's blog or my own personal blog.
3 I will post the Company's legal disclaimer on my Company-owned business blog and my own personal blog. The Company's legal disclaimer reads: "The postings on this blog are my own and do not necessarily reflect the opinions, positions, or strategies of my employer, The Company."

4. I will abide by the Company's Sexual Harassment and Discrimination Policy in all blog posts, business-related and personal.

5. I will adhere to the Company's Electronic Communications Policy, including language and content guidelines as well as other rules, in all blog posts, business-related and personal.

6. I will comply with the Company's Code of Ethics in all blog posts, business-related and personal.

7. I will adhere to the Company's Blog Policy and Procedures in all blog posts, business-related and personal.

8. I will treat readers and commenters with professional respect.

9. I will reply to readers' e-mail messages in a timely and professional manner.

10. I will not engage in comment spam or splogging.

11. I will write in an honest, transparent, first-person style.

12. I will make every effort to ensure that my posts are 100 percent accurate and factual.

13. I will not post gossip, rumors, lies, falsehoods, defamatory comments, personal attacks, harassing, discriminatory, menacing, or otherwise inappropriate and offensive content that violates any of the Company's written policies.

14. I will be mindful of the fact that blog content creates written business records that may be retained for business, legal, and regulatory purposes.

15. I will not violate copyright law. I will secure permission of the copyright holder before publishing copyrighted material. I will cite sources and link to online references and source material.

16. I will adhere to the Company's Confidentiality Agreement. I will not post content that would violate the trade secrets, confidentiality, or privacy of the Company, its employees, executives, customers, business partners, suppliers, or other third parties.

17. I will comply with the Company's netiquette, or electronic etiquette, guidelines in all blog posts, business and personal.

18. I will strive to keep my posts well-written, mechanically correct, factually accurate, original, readable, and appealing to readers.

Violations and Disciplinary Action

Employees who violate the Company's Blog Policy may face disciplinary action, up to and including termination.

Employee Acknowledgment

If you have questions about the above Blog Policy, address them to the Blog Czar before signing the following agreement.

I have read the Company's Blog Policy and agree to abide by it. I understand that a violation of any of the above rules, policies, and procedures may result in disciplinary action, up to and including my termination.

_____   _____
Employee Name (Printed)   Employee Signature

_____

Date

© 2006, Nancy Flynn, The ePolicy Institute, www.ePolicyInstitute.com. For informational purposes only. No reliance should be placed on this without the advice of counsel. Individual blog and electronic policies should be developed with assistance from competent legal counsel.

Blog Policy 2

The Company provides employees with external blog access, primarily for business purposes. Employees using the Company's external blog are responsible for behaving professionally, ethically, and responsibly in the blogosphere. To that end, the Company has established the following Blog Policy.

Employees are required to adhere to the Company's Blog Policy when at the office (or elsewhere) using the Company's business blog system for business or personal reasons. Employees also are expected to comply with the Company's Blog Policy when at home (or elsewhere) using a personal blog for business or personal reasons.

Violations of the Company's Blog Policy, whether they occur on the Company's blog or the employee's own personal blog, will result in disciplinary action, up to and including termination.

1. Employee-bloggers are required to write under their own names, whether using a company-hosted business blog or a personal blog. Pseudonyms and anonymous postings are prohibited.
2. Employee bloggers are required to identify themselves, by name and title, as employees of the Company, whether using a company-hosted business blog or a personal blog.

3. Employee-bloggers must incorporate the following legal disclaimer into their business and personal blogs: "The opinions expressed on this blog are my own personal opinions. They do not reflect the opinions of my employer, the Company."

4. Employee-bloggers are prohibited from attacking, defaming, harassing, discriminating against, menacing, threatening, or otherwise exhibiting inappropriate or offensive behavior or attitudes toward coworkers, supervisors, executives, customers, vendors, shareholders, the media, other bloggers, or other third parties, whether using a company-hosted business blog or a personal blog.

5. Employee-bloggers are prohibited from disclosing confidential, sensitive, proprietary, secret, or private information about the Company, employees, executives, customers, business partners, suppliers, or other third parties, whether using a company-hosted business blog or a personal blog.

6. Employee-bloggers are prohibited from disclosing financial information about the Company without permission from the investor relations department, whether using a company-hosted business blog or a personal blog. This includes revenues, profits, forecasts, and other financial information.

7. Employee-bloggers may discuss the Company's competitors, but must do so in a respectful, professional manner, whether using a company-hosted business blog or a personal blog.

8. Employee-bloggers must adhere to the Company's written content and language guidelines, whether using a company-hosted business blog or a personal blog. Prohibited content includes, but is not limited to, obscene, profane, adult-oriented, pornographic, harassing, discriminatory, menacing, threatening, and otherwise offensive text, art, photos, videos, graphics, cartoons, and other content.

9. Employee-bloggers are prohibited from posting copyright-protected material without the express, written permission of the copyright owner, whether using a company-hosted business blog or a personal blog.

10. Employee-bloggers must comply with all of the Company's written rules and policies, including but not limited to the Company's Blog Policy, Sexual Harassment and Discrimination Policy, Ethics Guidelines, Code of Conduct, and Electronic Communications Policy, whether using a company-hosted business blog or a personal blog.

11. Violation of the Company's Blog Policy (or any other Company policy) will result in disciplinary action, up to and including termi-

nation, whether using a company-hosted business blog or a personal blog.

Acknowledgment and Signature

If you have any questions about the above Blog Policy, address them to the human resources director before signing the following agreement.

I have read the Company's Blog Policy and agree to abide by it. I understand that a violation of any of the above rules, policies, and procedures may result in disciplinary action, up to and including my termination.

_____   _____
User Name   User Signature

_____
Date

© 2006, Nancy Flynn, The ePolicy Institute, www.ePolicyInstitute.com. For informational purposes only. No reliance should be placed on this without the advice of counsel. Individual blog and electronic policies should be developed with assistance from competent legal counsel.

Blog Policy 3

The Company provides employees with external blog access primarily for business purposes. Employees who engage in business or personal blogging during work hours are required to adhere to the rules, policies, and procedures listed below. Employees who engage in personal blogging in their own homes or elsewhere during nonwork hours also are required to adhere to the rules, policies, and procedures listed below. Violations of the Company's Blog Policy, whether they occur on the Company's blog or the employee's own personal blog, will result in disciplinary action, up to and including termination.

Anonymity: Employees are prohibited from blogging under a false name or identity. Employees are required to identify themselves as employees of the Company on Company-sponsored business blogs. If you choose to identify yourself as an employee of the Company on your own personal blog, please be aware that readers may view you as a de facto spokesperson for the company. Please act accordingly and in compliance with these policies and procedures.

Links: Incoming and outgoing links help make blogs more relevant and appealing to readers. When you see a relevant post, site, survey, article,

or other material, consider linking to it. Be sure to observe copyright laws when linking to copyright-protected information. Employees are prohibited from linking to material that is obscene, harassing, discriminatory, menacing, threatening, unlawful, unethical, or in any way violates any of the Company's employment policies. When using company-sponsored blogs, employees are prohibited from clicking on links in comment spam and splogs.

Confidentiality: A trade secret has value only if it remains a secret. When you blog at work, adhere to the Company's rules and policies governing confidentiality, trade secrets, intellectual property, proprietary information, and privacy. Employees who operate a personal blog outside the office are prohibited from writing about the Company or any company-related matter including but not limited to employees and executives, events, transactions, products, services, competitors, suppliers, confidential information, trade secrets, intellectual property, etc. Employees who operate a personal blog outside the office are prohibited from publishing the Company's logos, trademarks, slogans, advertisements, printed literature, commercials, videos, podcasts, or any other company-owned content.

Be professional. Be conversational. Put a human face on the Company. Your business and personal blog posts and comments reflect on your professionalism and the Company's credibility. In spite of the blogosphere's informal nature, employees are expected to write responsibly. Adhere to the Company's content, language, ethics, harassment, and discrimination guidelines. Adhere to the Company's netiquette rules. Make sure all blog posts are mechanically and grammatically correct.

Investor Relations: Employees are forbidden to post content related to the Company's financials, including but not limited to revenue, earnings, sales, projections, future plans, inventories, strategies, and share price.

Media Relations: All media requests should be routed to the Company's media relations director. Employees are not permitted to respond to media inquiries, conduct interviews, provide background material, or otherwise engage in media relations activities without the permission of the media relations director.

Copyright Adherence: Employees are not permitted to post, copy, transfer, rename, and/or edit copyright-protected material without permission of the owner. Employees may not link to copyright-protected content without permission of the copyright holder. Copyright infringement may result in disciplinary action, up to and including termination, as well as legal action by the copyright owner.

Appropriate Content: Employees are responsible for the content of all blog posts including text, audio, photos, videos, and other images.

Fraudulent, harassing, discriminatory, menacing, threatening, obscene, or otherwise inappropriate and objectionable content is prohibited. When blogging, employees are required to comply with all Company policies, rules, and guidelines including but not limited to Blog Policy, Electronic Communications Policy, Ethics Guidelines, Sexual Harassment and Discrimination Policy, Code of Conduct, Non-Disclosure/Confidentiality Agreement, and Netiquette Rules.

Privacy & Security: All blog posts published on the Company's blog system are the property of the organization, and should be considered public information. The Company reserves the right to access and monitor all blog posts, comments, and archives on the organization's system as deemed necessary and appropriate. Blog content is public, not private, communication. All blog posts and comments, including text and images, can be disclosed to law enforcement or other third parties without prior consent of the employee who sent or received the information.

Monitoring: Employees have no reasonable expectation of privacy when using the Company's blog system. The Company reserves the right to access and monitor all blog posts, comments, and archives on the organization's system as deemed necessary and appropriate. In addition, the Company reserves the right to monitor the blogosphere as a whole, including personal blogs that are operated by employees during nonwork hours, in their own homes or elsewhere. Blog content is public, not private, communication. Violations of the Company's Blog Policy—or any other Company rule, policy, guideline, or code—will result in disciplinary action, up to and including termination, regardless of whether the violation occurs on a company-hosted blog or the employee's own personal blog.

Sexual Harassment & Discrimination: The Company prohibits the publication of blog posts and comments that are in any way harassing or discriminatory. Employees are prohibited from posting derogatory and/or inflammatory remarks—including but not limited to jokes, rumors, gossip, innuendos, and defamatory comments—about sex, sexual preference, sexual orientation, race, religion, national origin, physical attributes, and/or ethnic background. Violations of the Company's Sexual Harassment and Discrimination Policy—or any other Company rule, policy, guideline, or code—will result in disciplinary action, up to and including termination, regardless of whether the violation occurs on a company-hosted blog or the employee's own personal blog.

Netiquette Rules: Employees must adhere to the rules of blog etiquette, or netiquette. In other words, you must be polite, adhere to the organization's content rules, and blog in an appropriate, legal, and ethical manner.

Disclaimer: Employees are required to post this legal disclaimer on their business and personal blogs: "The views expressed on this blog are my own and do not necessarily reflect the views of my employer, the Company."

Violations: This Blog Policy is intended to provide Company employees with general examples of acceptable and unacceptable use of the Company's blog system, as well as employees' own personal blogs. A violation of these rules and policies may result in disciplinary action, up to and including termination.

Acknowledgment: If you have questions about the above Blog Policy, address them to the Blog Czar before signing the following agreement.

I have read the Company's Blog Policy and agree to abide by it. I understand that a violation of any of the above rules, policies, and procedures may result in disciplinary action, up to and including my termination.

_____   _____

User Name   User Signature

_____

Date

NOTES

Chapter 1

1. Stephen Baker and Heather Green, "Blogs Will Change Your Business," *Business-Week Online* (May 2, 2005), www.businessweek.com.
2. "One Blog Created 'Every Second,'" *BBC News* (August 2, 2005), http://news .bbc.co.uk/go/pr/fr/-/1/hi/technology/4737671.stm. See also *"State of the Blogosphere, August 2005, Part 1: Blog Growth,"* Technorati Weblog, www .technorati.com/weblog/2005/08/34.html.
3. "The State of Blogging," Pew Internet & American Life Project Data Memo (January 2005).
4. Maryanne Murray Buechner, "50 Coolest Websites 2005: Blogs," Time Online (June 20, 2005), www.time.com.
5. www.bloggies.com.
6. Daniel Lyons, "Attack of the Blogs," *Forbes* (November 14, 2005), www.forbes .com.
7. "'Blog' Tops List of Dictionary Requests," *Columbus Dispatch* (December 6, 2004)
8. Baker and Green, "Blogs Will Change Your Business."
9. "Blogging in the Enterprise: A Guidewire Group Market Cycle Survey," sponsored by iUpload (October 2005), www.iupload.com.
10. Sarah E. Needleman, "Blogging Becomes a Corporate Job; Digital 'Handshake'?" *The Wall Street Journal* (May 31, 2005).
11. "HP Surveys Nation's Small Businesses to Learn What Fuels the Engines of Today's Economy," HP Press Release (April 27, 2005), www.hp.com.
12. Needleman, "Blogging Becomes a Corporate Job."
13. Excerpted from author Nancy Flynn's telephone interview with Brian Doyle, IBM's director of corporate affairs, November 14, 2005.
14. Sarah Kellogg, "Do You Blog?" *Washington Lawyer* (April 2005), www.dcbar.org.
15. Baker and Green, "Blogs Will Change Your Business."
16. Needleman, "Blogging Becomes a Corporate Job."
17. David Kirkpatrick and Daniel Roth, "Why There's No Escaping The Blog," *Fortune* (January 10, 2005).

18. "One Blog Created 'Every Second.'"
19. "Blogging in the Enterprise."
20. "HP Surveys Nation's Small Businesses."
21. "One Blog Created 'Every Second.'"
22. Ibid.
23. Corporate Blogging. Info, 2005, www.corporateblogging.info/basics/why, as reported by "New Frontiers In Employee Communications, 2005," Edelman, www.edelman.com.
24. Vauhini Vara, "New Search Engines Help Users Find Blogs," *The Wall Street Journal* (September 7, 2005), www.wsj.com.
25. Stephanie Armour, "Warning: Your Clever Little Blog Could Get You Fired," *USA Today* (June 15, 2005). See also "The State of Blogging."
26. Ibid.
27. "The State of Blogging."
28. Needleman, "Blogging Becomes A Corporate Job."
29. "HP Surveys Nation's Small Businesses."
30. Kirkpatrick and Roth, "Why There's No Escaping the Blog."
31. "Blogging in the Enterprise."
32. "Engaging the Blogosphere" survey, October 2005, Edelman and Technorati, www.edelman.com.
33. Kirkpatrick and Roth, "Why There's No Escaping the Blog."
34. Lev Grossman, "Meet Joe Blog," *Time* (June 21, 2004).
35. Ibid.
36. Ibid.
37. "One Blog Created 'Every Second.'"
38. Vara, "New Search Engines Help Users Find Blogs."
39. Ibid.
40. "The State of Blogging."
41. Kirkpatrick and Roth, "Why There's No Escaping the Blog."

Chapter 2

1. David Kirkpatrick and Daniel Roth, "Why There's No Escaping the Blog," *Fortune*, January 10, 2005.
2. "2004 Workplace E-Mail and Instant Messaging Survey," American Management Association and The ePolicy Institute, www.epolicyinstitute.com.
3. "2005 Electronic Monitoring and Surveillance Survey," American Management Association and The ePolicy Institute, www.epolicyinstitute.com.
4. "Talking from the Inside Out: The Rise of Employee Bloggers," Edelman and Intelliseek (Fall 2005). See also "Edelman 2005 New Frontiers in Employee Communications Survey," www.edelman.com.
5. "2005 Electronic Monitoring and Surveillance Survey."
6. "One Blog Created 'Every Second,'" *BBC News* (August 2, 2005), http://news.bbc.co.uk/go/pr/fr/-/1/hi/technology/4737671.stm. See also *"State of the Blogosphere, August 2005, Part 1: Blog Growth,"* Technorati Weblog, www.technorati.com/weblog/2005/08/34.html.

7. Vauhini Vara, "New Search Engines Help Users Find Blogs," *The Wall Street Journal Online* (September 7, 2005), www.wsj.com.

8. "Talking from the Inside Out." See also "Edelman 2005 New Frontiers in Employee Communications Survey," www.edelman.com

9. "2005 Electronic Monitoring and Surveillance Survey."

10. Ibid.

11. "Talking from the Inside Out."

12. Arianna Huffington, "Come on in, the blogging's wonderful," *TimesOnline* (May 15, 2005), http://business.timesonline.co.uk.com. See also www.huffingtonpost.com.

13. "No Longer Safe for Work: Blogs," *Wired News* (October 24, 2005), www.wired news.com.

14. Ibid.

15. "Engaging the Blogosphere," An Edelman/Technorati Study (October 2005), www.extranet.edelman.com/bloggerstudy.

16. Ibid.

17. Daniel Lyons, "Attack of the Blogs," *Forbes* (November 14, 2005), www.forbes .com.

18. "Blogging in the Enterprise: A Guidewire Group Market Cycle Survey," sponsored by iUpload (October 2005).

19. Bradley Johnson, "What Blogs Cost American Business," *Ad Age* (October 24, 2005), www.adage.com.

20. Dan Malachowski, "Wasted Time at Work Costing Companies Billions." Report on America Online/Salary.com's 2005 productivity survey, www.salary.com.

Chapter 3

1. Stephen Baker and Heather Green, "Blogs Will Change Your Business," *BusinessWeek Online* (May 2, 2005), www.businessweek.com.

2. Sarah E. Needleman, "Blogging Becomes a Corporate Job; Digital 'Handshake'?" *The Wall Street Journal* (May 31, 2005).

3. "Blogging in the Enterprise: A Guidewire Group Market Cycle Survey," sponsored by iUpload (October 2005).

4. "Engaging the Blogosphere," An Edelman/Technorati Study (October 2005), www.edelman.com.

5. "Blogging in the Enterprise."

6. Ibid.

7. Ibid.

8. Ibid.

9. Ibid.

10. Baker and Green, "Blogs Will Change Your Business."

11. Jonathan Schwartz, "If You Want to Lead, Blog," *Harvard Business Review* (November 2005), www.hbr.org.

12. Tip submitted to the author by David Carter of iUpload (November 11, 2005), www.iupload.com.

13. "Engaging the Blogosphere," An Edelman/Technorati Study (September 2005). See also "2005 Edelman Trust Barometer."

14. Tania Ralli, "Brand Blogs Capture the Attention of Some Companies," *The New York Times* (October 24, 2005), www.nytimes.com.

15. "US: 51% of Journalists Use Blogs," *The Editors Weblog* (August 2005), www .editorsweblog.org. See also Janet Johnson, "Gross Blog Anatomy: Dissecting Blogs From a Marketer's Perspective, Marqui Whitepaper (2005), blog.marqui .com.

16. Matt Villano, "Write All About It (At Your Own Risk)," *The New York Times* (July 24, 2005).

17. "Corporate Blogging: Is It Worth the Hype?" Backbone Media, Inc. Survey (2005), www.backbonemedia.com/blogsurvey.

Chapter 4

1. "Brand Rehab: How Corporations Can Restore a Tarnished Image," *Marketing Wharton*, www.knowledge.wharton.upenn.edu.

2. Excerpted from author Nancy Flynn's phone interview with Attorney Stephen M. Fronk of Howard Rice Nemerovski Canady Falk & Rabkin, www.howard rice.com (October 12, 2005).

3. "Talking from the Inside Out: The Rise of Employee Bloggers." White paper sponsored by Edelman and Intelliseek (2005), www.edelman.com.

4. David Kirkpatrick and Daniel Roth, "Why There's No Escaping the Blog," *Fortune* (January 10, 2005).

5. Excerpted from author Nancy Flynn's telephone interview with attorney Stephen M. Fronk, Howard Rice Nemerovski Canady Falk & Rabkin, www.howardrice .com (October 12, 2005).

6. Excerpted from author Nancy Flynn's telephone interview with Christine Halvorson of Stonyfield Farm (October 7, 2005), www.stonyfield.com.

Chapter 5

1. David Kirkpatrick and Daniel Roth, "Why There's No Escaping the Blog," *Fortune* (January 10, 2005).

2. Nancy Flynn and Randolph Kahn, Esq., *E-Mail Rules,* New York, AMACOM, 2003.

3. Michele Schroeder, "Emerging Law: State & Federal Statutes Address E-Discovery," *Digital Discovery & E-Evidence* (January 2002), www.krollontrack.com. See also Nancy Flynn, *Instant Messaging Rules*, New York, AMACOM, 2004.

4. "Document Retention & Destruction Policies for Digital Data," Applied Discovery White Paper, www.lexisnexis.com/applieddiscovery.

5. "2004 Workplace E-Mail and Instant Messaging Survey," conducted by American Management Association and The ePolicy Institute. Survey findings available at www.epolicyinstitute.com.

6. Christopher D. Wall and Michele C. S. Lange, "Recent Developments in Electronic Discovery," *Washington Lawyer* (March 2003). See also Nancy Flynn, *Instant Messaging Rules*, New York, AMACOM, 2004.

7. Flynn and Kahn, *E-Mail Rules.*

8. "2004 Workplace E-Mail and Instant Messaging Survey," American Management Association and The e-Policy Institute.

9. *Coleman (Parent) Holdings, Inc. v. Morgan Stanley & Co., Inc.,* 2005 WL 679071 (Fla. Cir. Ct., March 1, 2005). See also "Case Law Update and E-Discovery News," vol. 5, issue 1, first quarter 2006, Kroll Ontrack, www.krollontrack.com.

10. "Case Law Update and E-Discovery News," vol. 5, issue 1, first quarter 2006, Kroll Ontrack, www.krollontrack.com.

11. *United States v. Philip Morris, USA, Inc.,* No. Civ. A. 99-2496, 2004 WL 1627252 (D.D.C. July 21, 2004). See also "Electronic Discovery and Evidence," http://arkfeld.blogs.com.

12. "Document Retention & Destruction Policies for Digital Data," Applied Discovery White Paper, www.lexisnexis.com/applieddiscovery.

13. "Top 10 Tips for Effective Electronic Records Management," Kroll Ontrack, www.krollontrack.com. See also Nancy Flynn, *Instant Messaging Rules,* New York, AMACOM, 2004.

14. "2004 Workplace E-Mail and Instant Messaging Survey."

15. Excerpted from author Nancy Flynn's phone interview with David Carter, iUpload's CTO and VP, Strategy (November 11, 2005), www.iUpload.com.

16. Michael Osterman, "A Legal Guide to E-Mail Retention," *Network World Messaging Newsletter* (February 4, 2002), www.nwfusion.com. See also Nancy Flynn, *Instant Messaging Rules,* New York, AMACOM, 2004.

17. Flynn and Kahn, *E-Mail Rules.*

Chapter 6

1. Daniel Lyons, "Attack of the Blogs," *Forbes* (November 14, 2005), www.forbes.com.

2. Paul Starkman, "Mixed Verdicts," *Law Technology News* (November 2005), www.lawtechnologynews.com.

3. Ibid.

4. Excerpted from author Nancy Flynn's phone interview with attorney Stuart Levi of Skadden, Arps, Slate, Meagher & Flom LLP, www.skadden.com (October 12, 2005).

5. Excerpted from author Nancy Flynn's phone interview with attorney Stephen M. Fronk of Howard Rice Nemerovski Canady Falk & Rabkin, www.howardrice.com (October 12, 2005).

6. Ibid.

7. Nancy Flynn and Randolph Kahn, Esq., *E-Mail Rules,* New York, AMACOM, 2003.

8. "Employee Blogging," *Covington & Burling Technology & Software E-Alert* (April 18, 2005), www.cov.com.

9. *Blakey v. Continental Airlines, Inc.,* 164 N.J. 38, 751 A.2d 538, 2000 N.J. Lexis 650 (N.J. 2000). Paul Starkman, "Mixed Verdicts," *Law Technology News* (November 2005), www.lawtechnologynews.com.

10. William A. Clineburg, Jr., and Peter N. Hall, "Addressing Blogging by Employees," *The National Law Journal* (June 6, 2005), www.law.com.

11. *Immunomedics, Inc. v. Doe*, 324 N.J. Super. 160, 775 A.2d 773 (N.J. App. Div. 2001). Paul Starkman, "Mixed Verdicts," *Law Technology News* (November 2005), www.lawtechnologynews.com.

12. "Reprieve for Anonymous Blogger," CBS News (October 6, 2005), www.CBS News.com/stories/2005/10/06/tech/main923134.shtml.

13. "Defending Your Company Against 'Cybersmear,'" Sachnoff & Weaver Archived Client Advisories (September 19, 2002), www.sachnoff.com.

14. "Blogging in the Enterprise," A Guidewire Group Market Cycle Survey sponsored by iUpload (October 2005), www.iupload.com.

15. Flynn and Kahn, *E-Mail Rules*.

Chapter 7

1. Stephen Baker and Heather Green, "Blogs Will Change Your Business," *Business-Week Online* (May 2, 2005), www.businessweek.com.

2. Nancy Flynn, *Instant Messaging Rules*, New York, AMACOM, 2004.

3. Excerpted from author Nancy Flynn's phone interview with attorney Stephen Fronk, Howard Rice Nemerovski Canady Falk & Rabkin (October 12, 2005), www.howardrice.com.

4. *Bartnicki v. Vopper*, 532 U.S. 514, 121 S. Ct. 1389, 152 L.Ed.2d 532 (2001). Paul Starkman, "Mixed Verdicts," *Law Technology News* (November 2005), www.law technologynews.com.

5. Excerpted from author Nancy Flynn's telephone interview with attorney David Snead, www.dsnead.com (October 13, 2005).

6. Excerpted from author Nancy Flynn's telephone interview with attorney Doug Isenberg, GigaLaw.com (October 14, 2005).

7. Ibid. See also David Snead, "DMCA—Digital Millennium Copyright Act," www.dsnead.com.

8. Excerpted from author Nancy Flynn's interview with attorney David Snead. Also, excerpted from author Nancy Flynn's phone interview with attorney Stephen Fronk, Howard Rice Nemerovski Canady Falk & Rabkin (October 12, 2005), www.howardrice.com.

Chapter 8

1. Daniel Lyons, "Attack of the Blogs," *Forbes* (November 14, 2005), www.forbes .com.

2. Excerpted from author Nancy Flynn's telephone interview with attorney Stephen M. Fronk, Howard Rice Nemerovski Canady Falk & Rabkin, www.howardrice .com (October 12, 2005)

3. Ibid.

4. Christopher Null, "No Longer Safe for Work: Blogs," *Wired News* (October 24, 2005), www.wired.com.

5. "Electronic Discovery and Evidence," http://arkfeld.blogs.com/ede/2005/02/ jp-morgan-pays-html.

6. "State Street Research Reaches Settlement with NASD Relating to Supervision of Excessive Trading," State Street Research press release distributed via Business Wire (February 19, 2004).

7. "EX Product Family for Financial Services," Legato Power Point Presentation (2004).

8. Excerpted from author Nancy Flynn's phone interview with attorney Stephen Fronk, Howard Rice Nemerovski Canady Falk & Rabkin (October 12, 2005), www.howardrice.com.

9. "62% of Employees Report Incidents at Work That Put Customer Data at Risk for Identity Theft," Vontu press release announcing Harris Intereactive/Vontu Survey (June 2, 2003), www.vontu.com/news.

10. "2004 Workplace E-Mail and IM Survey," sponsored by American Management Association and The ePolicy Institute. Survey summary available at www.epolicy institute.com.

11. Jeff Brandes, "The Role of Secure Archiving in the E-Mail Life Cycle," Infostor (November 2003), www.infostor.com.

Chapter 9

1. Amy Joyce, "Free Expression Can Be Costly When Bloggers Bad-Mouth Jobs," Washington Post (February 11, 2005), www.washingtonpost.com. See also William A. Clineburg, Jr. and Peter N. Hall, "Addressing Blogging by Employees," The National Law Journal (June 6, 2005), www.nlj.com.

2. "2005 Electronic Monitoring and Surveillance Survey," sponsored by American Management Association and The ePolicy Institute. Survey summary available at www.epolicyinstitute.com.

3. "Talking from the Inside Out: The Rise of Employee Bloggers," Report sponsored by Edelman and Intelliseek (2005), www.edelman.com.

4. "2005 Electronic Monitoring and Surveillance Survey."

5. Ibid.

6. Paul Starkman, "Mixed Verdicts," Law Technology News (November 2005), www.lawtechnologynews.com.

7. "IBM Blogging Policy and Guidelines," IBM Corporation (May 16, 2005), www.ibm.com.

8. Starkman, "Mixed Verdicts."

9. Anna-Maria Mende, "US: 51% of Journalists Use Blogs," The Editors Weblog (August 26, 2005), www.editorsweblog.org.

10. Jo Best, "UK Staff in the Dark on Blogs," Silicon.com (September 27, 2005).

11. Starkman, "Mixed Verdicts."

Chapter 10

1. David P. Willis, "Bloggers Beware," Asbury Park Press (September 26, 2005). Automobile Club of Southern California spokeswoman Carol Thorp quoted, www.app.com.

2. "2004 Workplace E-Mail and Instant Messaging Survey," sponsored by American Management Association and The ePolicy Institute. Survey summary available online at www.epolicyinstitute.com.
3. "2001 Electronic Policies and Practices Survey," conducted by American Management Association, *U.S. News & World Report,* The ePolicy Institute. Survey findings available online at www.epolicyinstitute.com.
4. Nancy Flynn and Randolph Kahn, Esq., *E-Mail Rules,* New York, AMACOM, 2003.

Chapter 11

1. Excerpted from author Nancy Flynn's interview with Stonyfield Farm's Chief Blogger and Web Editor/Writer Christine Halvorson (October 7, 2005), www .stonyfield.com.
2. Sarah E. Needleman, "Blogging Becomes a Corporate Job; Digital 'Handshake'?" *The Wall Street Journal* (May 31, 2005).
3. Ibid.
4. "Generation Y Defined," Onpoint Marketing & Promotions, www.onpoint-marketing.com.
5. David Kirkpatrick and Daniel Roth, "Why There's No Escaping the Blog," *Fortune* (January 10, 2005).
6. Ibid.
7. Based on author Nancy Flynn's interview with Stonyfield Farm's Chief Blogger and Web Editor/Writer Christine Halvorson (October 7, 2005), www.stony field.com.
8. www.stonyfield.com/aboutus.
9. "Online Extra: Stonyfield Farm's Blog Culture," *BusinessWeek Online* (May 2, 2005), www.businessweek.com.
10. Excerpted from author Nancy Flynn's interview with Stonyfield Farm's Chief Blogger and Web Editor/Writer Christine Halvorson (October 7, 2005), www .stonyfield.com.
11. "Online Extra: Stonyfield Farm's Blog Culture," *BusinessWeek Online* (May 2, 2005), www.businessweek.com.
12. Ibid.
13. Ibid.
14. Excerpted from Flynn's interview with Christine Halvorson.
15. Excerpted from "Blog Best Practices" and "A Dozen Reasons to Consider Blogging," presented by Stonyfield Farm's Christine Halvorson as part of *PR Week*'s Webcast "Guide to Corporate Blogging," (July 21, 2005).

Chapter 12

1. David Kirkpatrick and Daniel Roth, "Why There's No Escaping the Blog," *Fortune* (January 10, 2005).
2. "Blogging in the Enterprise: A Guidewire Group Market Cycle Survey," sponsored by iUpload (October 2005), www.iUpload.com.

3. "2004 Workplace E-Mail and Instant Messaging Survey," Sponsored by American Management Association and The ePolicy Institute. Survey summary available online at www.epolicyinstitute.com.

4. Excerpted from "Blog Best Practices" and "A Dozen Reasons to Consider Blogging," presented by Stonyfield Farm's Christine Halvorson as part of *PR Week*'s webcast "Guide to Corporate Blogging," (July 21, 2005).

5. "Blogging in the Enterprise."

Chapter 13

1. Jessica Cutler, "Senator Sacked Me Over Tales of Congress," *The Guardian* (June 2, 2004), www.guardian.co.uk.

2. "Ad Man Quits After Sexist Speech," CBS News (October 23, 2005), www.cbs news.com.

3. Ibid.

4. "Notebook," *Time* (October 31, 2005).

5. Stephanie Armour, "Warning: Your Clever Little Blog Could Get You Fired," *USA Today*, (June 15, 2005).

6. "People Blog as Therapy, Says AOL," America Online, Inc. (AOL), www.aol .com.

7. David Fisher, "MP Warned on Name Calling," *The New Zealand Herald* (November 27, 2005), www.nzherald.co.nz.

8. Steven Elbow, "DePula Pleads Guilty to E-Mail Defamation," *Madison.com* (November 15, 2005), www.madison.com.

9. Ibid.

10. Ben Westhoff, "Attack of the Blog," *Riverfront Times* (December 22, 2004), www .riverfronttimes.com.

11. Charles Toutant, "Blog's Demise May Chill Other Federal Lawyers' Online Comments," *New Jersey Law Journal* (November 21, 2005), www.law.com.

12. Ibid.

13. Steve Johnson, "When Blogs Bite Back," *SignOnSanDiego.com* (November 14, 2005), http://signonsandiego.com.

14. Matt Villano, "Write All About It (At Your Own Risk), *The New York Times* (July 24, 2005).

15. Paul Starkman, "Mixed Verdicts," *Law Technology News* (November 2005), www .lawtechnologynews.com.

16. David Kirkpatrick and Daniel Roth, "Why There's No Escaping the Blog," *Fortune* (January 10, 2005).

17. www.marqui.com.

Chapter 14

1. Tim Bray, "Splogsplosion" (October 16, 2005), www.tbray.org.

2. CorporateBlogging.Info, 2005, www.corporateblogging.info/basics/why, as reported by "New Frontiers in Employee Communications, 2005," Edelman, www.edelman.com.

3. Stephanie Armour, "Warning: Your Clever Little Blog Could Get You Fired," *USA Today*, (June 15, 2005).

4. Elinor Mills, "Tempted by Blogs, Spam Becomes 'Splog.' " *CNET News.com* (October 20, 2005), www.news.com. See also Technorati's "State of the Blogosphere Report" (2005), www.technorati.com.

5. Ibid.

6. Yuki Noguchi, "A New Place for Spam's Old Pitches," *BizReport* (November 4, 2005), www.bizreport.com.

7. Bray, "Splogsplosion."

8. Mills, "Tempted by Blogs, Spam Becomes 'Splog.' "

9. Noguchi, "A New Place for Spam's Old Pitches."

10. Mills, "Tempted by Blogs, Spam Becomes 'Splog.' "

11. Ibid.

12. Nicole Lee, "How to Fight Those Surging Splogs," *Wired News* (October 27, 2005), www.wired.com.

13. Ibid.

14. Ibid.

Chapter 15

1. Matt Villano, "Write All About It (At Your Own Risk)," *The New York Times* (July 24, 2005).

2. "Talking from the Inside Out: The Rise of Employee Bloggers," Edelman and Intelliseek White Paper (Fall 2005), www.edelman.com.

3. "2005 Electronic Monitoring and Surveillance Survey," American Management Association and The ePolicy Institute, www.epolicyinstitute.com.

4. Villano, "Write All About It (At Your Own Risk)."

5. "The Bloggers' Rights Blog, http://rights.journalspace.com.

6. "Update 1: List of Fired Bloggers," *The Papal Bull* (January 12, 2005), http://homepage.mac.com/popemark/iblog/C2041067432/E372054822/

7. Curt Hopkins, "Statistics On Fired Bloggers," *Morpheme Tales* (December 28, 2004), www.morphemetales.blogspot.com.

8. "Delta Employee Fired for Blogging Sues Airline," *USA Today* (September 8, 2005), www.usatoday.com. See also *The Miami Herald* (Sept. 8, 2005), www.the miamiherald.com.

9. David P. Willis, "Bloggers Beware," *Asbury Park Press* (September 26, 2005), www.app.com.

10. Ibid.

11. April Witt, "Blog Interrupted," *The Washington Post* (August 15, 2004), www .washingtonpost.com. See also Richard Leiby, "The Hill's Sex Diarist Reveals All (Well, Some)," *The Washington Post* (May 23, 2004), www.washingtonpost.com.

12. Stephanie Armour, "Warning: Your Clever Little Blog Could Get You Fired," *USA Today* (June 15, 2005).

13. Jo Best, "Waterstone's Sacks Employee Over Blog," *Silicon.com* (January 10, 2005).

14. L. Lamor Williams, "Teacher Quits After Blog Probe Opens," *Star-Telegram.com* (October 15, 2005), www.dfw.com.

15. Stacey Burling, "A Blog Can Help You Stand Out, Sometimes to Your Detriment," Knight Ridder Newspapers (September 20, 2005). See also Patrick Giblin, "A Blog Can Help You Stand Out, Sometimes to Your Detriment," *Modesto Bee* (September 20, 2005), www.Modbee.com.
16. Ibid.
17. Anick Jesdanun, "Recent Firings Raise Issues for Workers Who Publish Blogs," *The Oregonian* (March 7, 2005), www.oregonline.com.
18. Armour, "Warning: Your Clever Little Blog Could Get You Fired."
19. Ibid.

Chapter 16

1. Jonathan Finer, "Teen Web Editor Drives Apple to Court Action," *Washington Post* (January 14, 2005), www.washingtonpost.com.
2. Ibid.
3. "Apple Targets Harvard Student for Product 'Leaks,'" TecWeb.com, *Information-Week* (January 13, 2005), www.informationweek.com.
4. Jarrett Murphy, "Site Precedent: What Apple Computer Insists Are 'Trade Secrets' These Websites Are Calling News," *Village Voice* (February 15, 2005), www.villagevoice.com.
5. Finer, "Teen Web Editor Drives Apple to Court Action."
6. www.thinksecret.com.
7. Finer, "Teen Web Editor Drives Apple to Court Action."
8. Ibid.
9. W. David Gardner, "Lawyer for Harvard Student Battling Apple Will Seek to Dismiss Lawsuit," *InformationWeek* (February 3, 2005), www.informationweek.com.
10. "Think Secret Goes on Offensive, Asks to Have Apple Lawsuit Dismissed," Think Secret press release, March 4, 2005, www.thinksecret.com.
11. Ibid.
12. Gardner, "Lawyer for Harvard Student Battling Apple Will Seek to Dismiss Lawsuit."
13. Finer, "Teen Web Editor Drives Apple to Court Action."
14. David Kesmodel, "Blogger Faces Lawsuit Over Comments by Readers," *The Wall Street Journal Online* (August 31, 2005).
15. "Traffic Power Lawsuit Update," *SEOBook.com* (September 15, 2005).
16. Kesmodel, "Blogger Faces Lawsuit Over Comments by Readers."
17. See SEOBook.com. See also www.nvd.uscourts.gov, case CV-S-05-1109-RLH-LRL.
18. Kesmodel, "Blogger Faces Lawsuit Over Comments by Readers."

Chapter 17

1. Steve Johnson, "When Blogs Bite Back," *The San Diego Union-Tribune, SignOn SanDiego.com* (November 14, 2005), http://signnonsandiego.com.

2. Holden Firth, "Businesses Begin to Court the Blogger's Vote," *TimesOnline* (September 26, 2005), www.business.timesonline.co.uk.

3. "Employee Blogging," Covington & Burling Technology & Software E-Alert, April 18, 2005, www.cov.com.

4. Anick Jesdanum, "Recent Firings Raise Issues for Workers Who Publish Blogs," *The Oregonian* (March 7, 2005), www.oregonline.com.

5. Matt Villano, "Write All About It (At Your Own Risk), *The New York Times* (July 24, 2005).

6. Alorie Gilbert, "FAQ: BLogging On The Job," *CNET News.com* (March 8, 2005), www.news.com.

7. "Employee Blogging," Covington & Burling Technology & Software E-Alert (April 18, 2005), www.cov.com.

8. Stephanie Armour, "Warning: Your Clever Little Blog Could get You Fired," *USA Today* (June 15, 2005).

9. David Kirkpatrick and Daniel Roth, "Why There's No Escaping The Blog," *Fortune* (January 10, 2005).

Chapter 18

1. Stephen Baker and Heather Green, "Blogs Will Change Your Business," *BusinessWeek Online* (May 2, 2005), www.businessweek.com.

2. Daniel Lyons, "Attack of the Blogs," *Forbes* (November 14, 2005), www.forbes.com.

3. Paul Durman, "Firms Line Up to Rocket Into The Blogosphere," *TimesOnline* (May 8, 2005), www.business.timesonline.co.uk.

4. Daniel Lyons, "Attack of the Blogs."

5. Anna-Maria Mende, "US: 51% of Journalists Use Blogs," *The Editors Weblog* (August 26, 2005), www.editorsweblog.org.

6. Philippe Naughton, "Murdoch Tells Editors to Embrace the Bloggers," *TimesOnline* (April 14, 2005), www.business.timesonline.co.uk.

7. "The State of Blogging," Pew Internet & American Life Project Data Memo (January 2005).

8. "New Frontiers in Employee Communications: 2005," Edelman Survey, (September 2005), www.edelman.com.

9. "Blogging in the Enterprise," a Guidewire Group Market Cycle Survey, sponsored by iUpload (October 2005), www.iupload.com.

10. "Engaging the Blogosphere," an Edelman/Technorati Study (October 2005), www.edelman.com.

11. Stephen Baker, "Bacon's Updates Media Guide With Blog Info" (October 26, 2005), www.blogspotting.net.

12. Daniel Lyons, "Attack of the Blogs," *Forbes* (November 14, 2005), www.forbes.com.

13. Mende, "US: 51% of Journalists Use Blogs."

Chapter 19

1. David Kirkpatrick and Daniel Roth, "Why There's No Escaping the Blog," *Fortune* (January 10, 2005).

2. Hillary Chura, "McDonald's Pulls Further Away From Mass Marketing," *Ad Age* *(June 16, 2004), www.adage.com.*

3. James Pethokoukis, "Spreading the Word," *U.S. News & World Report* (December 5, 2005), www.usnews.com.

4. Ibid.

5. "Sixth Annual Edelman Trust Barometer," (2005) www.edelman.com.

6. Tania Ralli, "Brand Blogs Capture the Attention of Some Companies," *The New York Times* (October 24, 2005), www.nytimes.com.

7. James Pethokoukis, "Spreading the Word," *U.S. News & World Report* (December 5, 2005), www.usnews.com.

8. Ibid.

9. "Branding 2.0," *AME Info* (September 18, 2005), www.aiminfo.com.

10. Ralli, "Brand Blogs Capture the Attention of Some Companies."

11. Pethokoukis, "Spreading the Word."

12. "Branding 2.0."

13. Ralli, "Brand Blogs Capture the Attention of Some Companies."

14. Ibid.

15. Kirkpatrick and Roth, "Why There's No Escaping The Blog."

16. Ibid.

17. "Marqui Pays Bloggers in Revolutionary Marketing Move," Marqui Press Release (December 2, 2004). See also "Marqui's Blogging Experience," www.marqui .com/paybloggers/

18. Janet Johnson, "Gross Blog Anatomy: Dissecting Blogs From A Marketer's Perspective," Marqui (2005), www.blog.marqui.com.

19. "Engaging the Blogosphere."

Chapter 20

1. Jonathan Schwartz, "If You Want to Lead, Blog," *Harvard Business Review* (November 2005), www.hbr.org.

2. "The State of Trust," *Sixth Annual Edelman Trust Barometer* (2005), www.edel man.com.

3. "New Frontiers in Employee Communications: 2005," Edelman Survey, www .edelman.com.

4. "The State of Trust."

5. "New Frontiers in Employee Communications: 2005," Edelman Survey, www .edelman.com.

6. Jonathan Schwartz, "If You Want to Lead, Blog."

7. Talking from the Inside Out: The Rise of Employee Bloggers." White paper sponsored by Edelman and Intelliseek (2005), www.edelman.com.

8. Janet Johnson, "Gross Blog Anatomy: Dissecting Blogs from a Marketer's Perspective," a Marqui Whitepaper (2005), www.blog.marqui.com.

9. Jonathan Schwartz, "If You Want to Lead, Blog."

10. iUpload InSights (April 12, 2005), http://hopper.iupload.com.

11. Schwartz, "If You Want to Lead, Blog."

12. "Talking from the Inside Out: The Rise of Employee Bloggers."

13. Ibid.

14. Edward Wong, "A Stinging Office Memo Boomerangs," *The New York Times* (April 5, 2001), C1. See also Nancy Flynn and Randolph Kahn, Esq., *E-Mail Rules*, New York, AMACOM, 2003.

15. J. Lynn Lunsford, Andy Pasztor, and Joann S. Lublin, "Boeing's CEO Forced to Resign Over His Affair with Employee," *The Wall Street Journal* (March 8, 2005).

16. "Blogging and Its Impact on Corporate Reputation," Cymfony White Paper (2005), www.cymfony.com.

17. "Engaging the Blogosphere," an Edelman/Technorati study (October 2005), www.edelman.com.

18. "Talking from the Inside Out."

19. "Democratization of Information," *Sixth Annual Edelman Trust Barometer* (2005), www.edelman.com.

Chapter 21

1. David Kirkpatrick and Daniel Roth, "Why There's No Escaping the Blog," *Fortune* (January 10, 2005).

2. Daniel Lyons, "Attack of the Blogs," *Forbes* (November 14, 2005), www.forbes.com.

3. Sarah E. Needleman, "Blogging Becomes A Corporate Job; Digital 'Handshake'?" *The Wall Street Journal* (May 31, 2005).

4. Lyons, "Attack of the Blogs."

5. Ibid.

6. "Engaging the Blogosphere," An Edelman/Technorati Study (October 2005), https://extranet.edelman.com/bloggerstudy.

7. Ibid.

8. Lydia Polgreen, "The Pen Is Mightier Than the Lock," *The New York Times* (September 17, 2004).

9. Kirkpatrick and Roth, "Why There's No Escaping the Blog."

10. Lyons, "Attack of the Blogs."

11. Polgreen, "The Pen Is Mightier Than the Lock."

12. Excerpted from author Nancy Flynn's telephone interview with Donna Tocci, Kryptonite public relations manager (November 11, 2005), www.kryptonite.com.

13. Ibid.

14. Ibid.

15. Kirkpatrick and Roth, "Why There's No Escaping the Blog."

16. Lyons, "Attack of the Blogs."

17. Ibid.

18. Polgreen, "The Pen Is Mightier Than the Lock."

19. Kirkpatrick and Roth, "Why There's No Escaping the Blog."

20. Ibid.

21. Excerpted from Flynn's telephone interview with Donna Tocci.

22. Ibid.

23. Ibid.

24. Ibid.

25. Ibid.

26. Ibid.

27. Ibid.

28. Lyons, "Attack of the Blogs."
29. "Engaging the Blogosphere."

Chapter 22

1. "Notebook," *Time* (October 31, 2005).
2. Kevin Newcomb, "McDonald's Dips Toe In Blogging Waters," *ClickZ Internet Advertising News* (October 18, 2005), www.clickz.com.
3. "Engaging the Blogosphere," An Edelman/Technorati Study (October 2005), https://extranet.edelman.com/bloggerstudy.
4. "The State of Blogging," Pew Internet & American Life Project Data Memo (January 2005).
5. "Engaging the Blogosphere," An Edelman/Technorati Study.
6. Ibid.
7. Ibid.
8. Ibid.

Chapter 23

1. "About IBM," www.ibm.com.
2. Excerpted from author Nancy Flynn's telephone interview with IBM's Brian Doyle, director of corporate affairs (November 14, 2005), www.ibm.com.
3. Ibid.

Chapter 25

1. "Welcome," www.edelman.com.
2. "Talking from the Inside Out: The Rise of Employee Bloggers," Edelman and Intelliseek (Fall 2005), www.edelman.com.
3. "Edelman 2005 New Frontiers in Employee Communications Survey," www.edelman.com.
4. "Engaging the Blogosphere: an Edelman/Technorati Study," (September 2005), www.extranet.edelman.com/bloggerstudy.
5. "Sixth Annual Edelman Trust Barometer: A Global Study of Opinion Leaders," Edelman (2005), www.edelman.com.
6. Excerpted from author Nancy Flynn's telephone interview with Christopher Hannegan, Edelman senior vice president and employee engagement practice director (October 18, 2005), www.edelman.com.
7. "Talking from the Inside Out: The Rise of Employee Bloggers."

Chapter 26

1. "Maintaining a Web Log," Edelman Principles & Code of Conduct (September 2005), www.edelman.com.

2. "Acknowledgement of Edelman's Code of Conduct," Edelman Principles & Code of Conduct (September 2005), www.edelman.com.

Glossary of Blog, Legal, and Technology Terms

1. Excerpted from author Nancy Flynn's telephone interview with Christopher Byrne of ControlsCaddy.com (November 11, 2005).
2. Lev Grossman, "Meet Joe Blog," *Time.com* (June 21, 2004).
3. "Branding 2.0," *AIM Info* (September 18, 2005), www.ameinfo.com.
4. "Defending Your Company Against 'Cybersmear,'" Sachnoff & Weaver Client Advisory, September 19, 2002, www.sachnoff.com.
5. James Pethokoukis, "Spreading the Word," *US News & World Report* (December 15, 2005), www.usnews.com.
6. James Pethokoukis, "Spreading the Word," *U.S. News & World Report* (December 5, 2005), www.usnews.com.
7. Adapted from Nancy Flynn and Randolph Kahn, Esq., *E-Mail Rules*, New York, AMACOM, 2003.
8. "Corporate Firewalls Blocking Blogs," Shel Holtz, *Webpronews.com*, October 26, 2005, www.webpronews.com.
9. "Legal Overview: The Electronic Frontier and the Bill of Rights," *Electronic Frontier Foundation* (April 4, 2005), www.eff.org/legal.
10. The Associated Press, "Firms Taking Action Against Worker Blogs," *New York Lawyer* (March 7, 2005), www.nylawyer.com.
11. Wayne Hurlbert, "Google Hub Sites: A Blog Goal," *Webpronews.com* (September 18, 2005), www.webpronews.com.
12. David Kirkpatrick and Daniel Roth, "Why There's No Escaping The Blog," *Fortune* (January 10, 2005).
13. "State of the Blogosphere" report from Technorati.
14. Jonathan Finer, "Teen Web Editor Drives Apple To Court Action," *Washington Post* (January 14, 2005), www.washingtonpost.com.

GLOSSARY OF BLOG, LEGAL, AND TECHNOLOGY TERMS

Aggregator: See RSS Aggregator.

Archive: A collection of the bloggers' past posts, organized and navigable by date. Typically a feature of blog publishing software.

AstroTurfing: Creating a fake grass roots movement in the blogosphere to generate awareness of or interest in a product or idea. Organizations pay consulting fees or otherwise encourage bloggers to create a buzz in the blogosphere by publishing fake posts or comments and hiding behind false identities.[1]

Blawg: A blog written by a lawyer or focused on legal issues.

Blog: Short for Weblog. The word blog, which was coined in 1997, works as both a noun and verb.[2] A blog is an online journal that contains written content, links, and photos, which are regularly updated. Blogs enable anyone with a computer and Internet access to publish their thoughts, ideas, and opinions for anyone else to read and comment upon. Some blogs are business-related, while others are highly personal. Some highly influential blogs boast an enormous public readership, while other blogs are intended strictly for a limited audience of friends and family.

Blogger: Someone who operates a blog.

Bloggerati: A variant of literati, bloggerati refers to the most prominent bloggers in the blogosphere.

Blogosphere: The universe of blogs, or Web logs. The community of bloggers.

Blogroll: A list of links to external sites (other blogs, bloggers, and Web-sites) that are favorites of or recommended by the blogger. The blogroll typically appears in a column on the homepage, rather than within the text of commentary. Helps form the community feeling of the blogosphere and encourages linking back and forth between sites.

Blogstorm: An attack in the blogosphere. A blogstorm typically occurs when one influential blogger alerts readers to a problem within an organization or a disturbing issue surrounding an individual, then others bloggers pile on. See Chapter 21 for examples of companies that have suffered high-profile, damaging blogstorms.

Blogware: Software used to publish and operate a blog.

Brand Bloggers: One step beyond customer evangelists, brand bloggers are "fanatics" who are devoted to writing (mainly positively, sometimes negatively) about their favorite brands on their own dedicated blogs, at their own expense, on their own time.[3]

Categories: Categories facilitate archiving of past blog entries. If a reader only wants to read posts related to one specific category ("blog policy," for example), the reader can review all the blogger's entries under "blog policy," and bypass all other, unrelated posts.

Citizen Journalists: People outside the traditional, mainstream news business who use blogs (their own or other's) to share newsworthy stories, provide analysis of news stories and events, and post or send newsworthy photos to mainstream media outlets.

Comments: Many blogs include a comment feature, which allows readers to easily and automatically respond to posts, ask questions, or inject their own point of view. Considered a vital element of a blog by blogging enthusiasts, many organizations fail to edit comments pre-post. Unedited comments can open an organization to claims of defamation, copyright infringement, and trade secret theft, among other risks.

Comment Spam: Blogs often provide comment sections to allow customers and other readers to add their own opinions and reactions to a post. Blog spammers use tools to automatically flood a blog with advertising in the form of bogus comments. Anything that's been spammed about in e-mail is probably being spammed in the blogosphere. A growing and serious problem for bloggers and blog platforms.

Communications Decency Act of 1996: Federal law that protects blog hosts, as neutral carriers of Internet content, from liability for anything posted on the blogs they host.[4]

Content Syndication: The way in which a blogger makes content, in all or in part, available for posting on other sites.

Corporate Evangelists: The process of identifying customers who are already crazy about your product or service, and are actively blogging about your organization, and turning them into customer evangelists who use their own blogs to spread the positive word about your company to others."[5]

Customer Evangelists: Superfans who are crazy about your product or service, and actively talking up your organization in their blogs. The organization turns superfans into customer evangelists by showering them with loads of personal attention, and motivating them to spread the good word about the company to others."[6]

Date/Time Stamps: A blogware feature that adds date and time stamps to individual posts. Helps with the organization and navigation of the blog archive. Also may be a valuable tool for the retention of blog business records, helping to support the accuracy and validity of a print out.

Dooced: To lose your job for the contents of your blog. Typically employee-bloggers are dooced because of negative or unflattering comments they have posted about their employers and or their companies' products or services. The term dooced was coined by blogger Heather B. Armstrong, who in 2002 was fired for writing about her job and colleagues on her site www.dooce.com.

Entry: See also "Post." The commentary, called an entry or post, that is written by a blogger on a blog. Some bloggers write multiple entries every day. Most entries are relatively short. Entries often include external links, and offer readers the opportunity to comment.

Filtering: The act of scanning and blocking access to blogs that may violate the organization's content policy or the content-related regulations of government and industry. The recommended approach is to establish written blog rules and policy first, then use software or an appliance tool to enforce your written guidelines.

Firewall: Software or hardware that automatically reviews network traffic and either blocks it or allows it to pass, based on content rules and policies. Firewalls typically sit between a private internal networks and the Internet and are common tools for protecting internal networks and users from harmful content and malicious intrusion.[7] Increasingly, organizations that are concerned about security, productivity, and other risks are using firewalls to block access to blogs.[8]

First Amendment: The First Amendment to the United States Constitution prohibits the government from abridging the freedom of speech.[9] Since the First Amendment only restricts government control of speech, private employers are free to fire at will in most states, provided the termination is not discriminatory or retaliation for whistle-blowing or union organizing.[10]

Hub Site: Achieving hub site status will elevate a blog to the top of the Google search engine rankings. A hub site is achieved by having large numbers of incoming and outgoing links. "Hubs are distinguished by their willingness to link out to other sites whose contents are based on similar themes."[11]

K-Log or Knowledge Blog: Typically, K-Logs are internal Intranet-based blogs uses as company communications/knowledge management cools.

Links: Successful bloggers strive to increase traffic and readership by incorporating incoming and outgoing links into their sites. Bloggers enhance the relevance of their blogs, and provide readers with a service, by including outgoing links to sites that contain relevant content or otherwise are likely to appeal to readers. High-quality content (a timely or controversial topic, compelling writing, and high search-engine rankings) helps motivate bloggers to create links into a site.

Moblogs: A Moblog, or mobile log, is a blog that can be updated remotely via camera phones or other mobile devices that transmit pictures and text.

MSM: Mainstream media. Through blogs, citizen journalists offer an alternative to the mainstream media.

News Aggregator: Also knows as an RSS Aggregator. A tool used to read RSS (Really Simple Syndication). See below.

Permalink: Contraction of "permanent link." The permalink creates a unique Web address for every posting on a blog. Bloggers link to one another's posts, which typically remain accessible forever via the permalink (unlike Web pages, which are subject to change). The permalink creates a double-edged sword for business, giving blogs "a viral quality, so a pertinent post can gain broad attention amazingly fast—and reputations can get taken down just as quickly."[12]

Photoblog: A blog that primarily contains photos, which are regularly updated and posted chronologically—just like text postings.

Ping: Ping services like Weblogs.com automatically alert (or "ping") subscribers when new content is added to a blog. That's one more good reason to update blog content regularly—ideally once a day.

Podcast: Contraction of "iPod" and "broadcasting." Poscasts are blog radio shows and audio or video recordings that are posted on a blog and broadcast over the Internet, or syndicated, via Really Simple Syndication (see RSS) to iPods, MP3 players, cell phones, and other mobile devices.

Post: See also "Entry." The commentary, called a post or entry, that is written by a blogger on a blog. Some bloggers post multiple times per day. Most posts are relatively short. Posts often include external links, and offer readers the opportunity to comment.

RSS (Really Simple Syndication or Rich Site Summary): (1) A way to notify readers that their favorite blogs have been updated with new content; and (2) a file format that allows anyone with a website to easily "syndicate" their content, so other sites can simply and automatically receive and reproduce excerpts, attributions, and links back to the originating website.

RSS Aggregator: Software or an online service that enables a blogger to read an RSS feed—new posts on a favorite blog. (Also called a reader or feedreader.)

RSS Feed: The file that contains a blog's latest posts. Read by an RSS aggregator, the RSS feed alerts readers when a blog has been updated. A time saver for readers, the RSS feed eliminates the need to visit blogs and Web sites for new information on selected topics. The RSS feed automatically brings the information to the reader.

Splog: Spam Blogs. Spam blogs do not provide any real content for users. Sploggers use automated tools to create fake blogs that are full of links to specific Web sites (generally sites selling goods and services). The goal of splogging is to boost search engine results and send traffic to the linked-to sites. Blog search engine Technorati estimates that 5.8 percent of new blogs, or about 50,000 posts, are fake or potentially fake.[13]

Tags: Categories or topics under which blog posts are organized. For example, a cat-lover's blog might feature that tags "kittens, adult cats, catnip, cat shelters, cat food, cat toys, veterinary care, etc. A click on any one of those tags will take you to posts that are related to the topic.

Trackbacks: Enables one blogger to connect to another blogger via a link. A method of notifying other bloggers that your post references one of their posts. Rather than leaving a comment on Blogger A's blog, Blogger B writes an entry on his own blog, with a link back to the source, Blogger A's blog.

Uniform Free Trade Secrets Act: Adopted by about 45 states, this act prevents third-parties (bloggers, for example) from knowingly exposing confidential information (a company's trade secrets, for example) from people who are bound by confidentiality agreements (employees, for example).[14]

Vicarious Liability: Under the legal principle known as vicarious liability, an employer may be held responsible for the accidental or intentional misconduct of employees. Employee-bloggers who post objectionable, offensive, or illegal content on a personal or business blogs could put their employers at risk of legal liability.

Vlog: Video blog. Distributing videos via blogs.

Wiki: A web site with pages that any reader may edit, adding pages, modifying content, or commenting on existing content. Primarily used by companies internally as a collaborative tool for employees. The term is adapted from the Hawaiian phrase "wiki wiki," which means "quick."

Web diary: A blog.

INDEX

221

ABOUT THE AUTHOR

Nancy Flynn is executive director of The ePolicy Institute, an organization dedicated to reducing employers' electronic risks and enhancing employees' electronic communications. An in-demand speaker and corporate trainer, she is the author of eight books published in four languages. Her books include *Instant Messaging Rules* (AMACOM 2004), *E-Mail Rules* (AMACOM 2003), *The ePolicy Handbook* (AMACOM 2001), and *Writing Effective E-Mail*. Flynn is a popular media source who has been featured in *Fortune, USA Today, Business Week, US News & World Report, The Wall Street Journal*, and *The New York Times*, as well as on CBS, CNN, CNBC, FOX, NPR, and other media outlets.

ePolicy Institute services include on-site and online seminars, expert witness services and litigation consulting, policy development and implementation, research surveys, and content development, including white papers and policy guides.

To schedule a training seminar or speaking engagement, book a consultation, or conduct a media interview, contact:

The ePolicy Institute
Nancy Flynn, Executive Director
614-451-3200
nancy@epolicyinstitute.com
www.epolicyinstitute.com